Dig Out Of Debt

Over 1000 of the Best Ideas from LivingOnADime.com

Would you like to learn how to save over $7000 in one year?

Simply go to www.LivingOnaDime.com and sign up for the free weekly newsletter.

You'll receive valuable money-saving tips that work, from the authors of this book.

Tawra Kellam and Jill Cooper are a mother daughter team who learned to live in difficult financial circumstances at a time in life when money was always in short supply. Living in a situation where they had to choose between one necessity and another really helped them gain a new perspective about the value of things. It also helped them make distinctions between needs and desires. Their goal is to educate people about better ways to handle money in the hope that the people they touch can live more fulfilled and less stressful lives.

For her entire life, *Tawra Kellam* has lived the frugal lifestyle. Her mother's determination to persevere through extraordinarily difficult financial circumstances is the basis of Tawra's frugal thinking.

Tawra, her husband and 4 children live in Colorado. In five years, they paid off $20,000 personal debt on an average income of $22,000 per year.

As a single mother of two, *Jill Cooper* started her own business without any capital and paid off $35,000 debt in 5 years on $1,000 a month income.

She then raised two teenagers alone on $500 a month income after becoming disabled with Chronic Fatigue Syndrome.

Table of Contents

Money Management

Grocery Savings

Cleaning Cents

Kids Cents

Debt Free Holidays

Money
Management

Are "THEY" ruining your finances?

Over the centuries human beings have been compared to sheep over and over again. I never cease to be amazed at how true that is. If one sheep decides to head down a road that goes right over a cliff, they all follow. Even in history when people march and demand the right to be individuals they still always seem to dress and act alike. Remember the "flower children" of the 60's. Even with their "free to be me" attitude, they were horrified if a man walked in with a suit and tie since it was different from what they would wear.

If children are doing drugs, drinking or just wearing strange outfits, they justify it because "everyone is doing it". So often, the parent's response is "If everyone jumps off a cliff that doesn't mean you should do it, too." Is that the story we tell them with our actions? Kids are very shrewd and have no tolerance for hypocrisy. We hurt our families and ourselves if we blindly follow the crowd. "They" (I still haven't figured out who "they" are but I don't think I like "them" or "their" ideas.) have set a standard of living that we must live by-- no matter what the cost.

They say you need a bigger house for the tax deduction. *They* say schools need to budget for palm pilots for students, even though *they* can't afford to pay the teachers. *They* say you need a big SUV so you'll be safe on the road.

"They" say you can't live on one income, so many moms who think it's best for their families if they stay home get jobs anyway because "they" say "You can't make it!" Never mind that the extra expense of childcare, work clothes and (for many) "guilt offerings" purchased for their kids often exceed the extra income. "They" say that's the way it's supposed to be.

How many dads have become only figures the kids wave good-bye to in the morning before heading off to two jobs because "they" say this is the world in which we live. Too many people who do this find that later in life their marriages are suffering, their kids are rebellious and resentful of their absence and the employer for whom they've invested all their time "providing" for the family lays them off.

"They" say you have to pay to send your children to college so they can become a success and make a lot of money. When did "they" come up with the idea that going to college makes a person successful? How many parents have accrued $40,000 in debt for their son or daughter's degree, only to find the student working in a field that has nothing to do with his degree? Certainly, a college education can be a useful tool, but it is one that is wasted if the student doesn't need it or fails to use it.

I find that the most successful human beings are those whose parents spent time with them and had the time to teach them values, self confidence, self reliance and love. You can always lose your stuff, but you can't lose your values or the knowledge that your parents love you.

Stop basing your financial decisions on what "they" think you should be doing. Financial worries are the biggest cause of stress for Americans, leading to all sorts of physical and emotional problems. These worries are almost always avoidable, but many choose the worries over the common sense.

The point of this story is not that you should never spend any money on anything. The point is that it is important that you decide whether or not spending your time or money some particular way is a good idea for your family. Keep in mind that when "they" tell you that you should do something, "they" are often trying to sell you something you don't really need.

Whenever you find yourself reflecting on your life and you realize you are doing something because "they" expect you to do it, decide for yourself what is really best for you and your family and do it!

THOUGHT OF THE DAY

By the time you can make ends meet, they move the ends.

Are You a Slave to Debt?
Land of the Free and Home of the Brave?

We Americans are proud of our freedom and our opposition to tyranny and slavery, but because of lack of self discipline, most of us are not free at all. We are enslaved by our emotions and our debt. Most of us would never consider agreeing to become indentured servants and yet, by our own lack of self discipline, many of us have sold ourselves into slavery. Have you ever thought about the fact that indentured servants usually had to work 7 years for their freedom and people who claim bankruptcy have black marks on their credit for 7 years?

By now all those well meaning New Year's resolutions have flown out the window, but don't despair: all is not completely lost. Here are a few money saving tips and ideas that will get you back on track, save you money and will actually work.

You say "But I don't know where to begin." Just begin. Don't over-think it. You don't need to be a rocket scientist to know that you have to stop spending more then you earn.

Have you ever told your child to go pick up the toys in their room only to have them start whining and crying, "But I don't know what to do." It's frustrating to hear that in a child because you and I both know an eight year old knows he's supposed to put his toys away and his dirty clothes in the hamper. He just doesn't want to do it. That whining and excuse making in an adult is even harder to take. As in a child, it's just an excuse to get out of doing something we don't want to do. Stop spending more then you earn.

Stop living a life of fear. Remember if you're an American you live in the land of the free and the home of the BRAVE. There are two things that always amaze me. The first is grown adults that cower before a child a quarter their size and who is throwing a fit while demanding to buy a toy. The second is to watch a grown adult cower when looking at a desk or table piled with papers and bills. It's just a bunch of paper, not a snake that is going to reach out and bite you. Be brave and start dealing with the papers and bills. Get them in order. Yes you may have to face some mistakes and things you don't want to think about, but do it anyway. Then get on with your life. Learn from your mistakes and don't make them again.

Here are a few suggestions to get that overwhelming pile of papers under control:

Quickly look at each paper and lay it into one of these 4 categories:

1. TRASH - Throw out and/or shred immediately.

2. FILES - Put in a box and set by file cabinet to sort and put in order some other day.

3. BILLS - Sort them in order by the date that they are due. If things are really out of control write down a list of all your bills and how much you owe. This will help give you a reality check of where you stand with your bills. You need to be brave and honest with this.

Using some common sense, start paying those bills. Pay your bills first. For a while, that may mean you have no money left for fun and entertainment, but that is the sacrifice you make for freedom.

4. CORRESPONDENCE - Put correspondence in a pile. Read and deal with it after you have your bill pile out of the way.

It's time to get angry and say enough is enough. I will no longer be enslaved and start fighting for my freedom from debt, even if my biggest enemy is myself!

Ever wonder about those people who spend $2.00 a piece on those little bottles of Evian water?

Try spelling Evian backwards: NAIVE

Frugal Ethics
When Frugal Becomes Just Plain Cheap

There are times when it's tempting to lie, steal or break one of the other 10 Commandments to get a good deal but, in living frugally, we all need to stick to being honest. This is not always easy to do, but I want to give some examples that may help you stay honest. Here are some common tactics that some people use that are unethical and sometimes illegal:

Stealing "Free" Merchandise - This one really irked me! We needed some labels for the business. UPS gives their customers free unlimited labels as needed for packing when shipping with UPS. We purchased labels from a lady on Ebay. When we received them, they arrived from the UPS shipping center. The lady told us that was her "other office"! What she did is take our money and then call UPS as if she were me and have them send me "free" labels. The gaul! I confronted her and reported it to UPS. I should have known it was a "too good to be true" deal! Incidentally, this particular lady had made tens of thousands of dollars on Ebay sales of UPS "free" labels. This is not only dishonorable, but illegal.

You need some pens because you are running short so you take a handful from a store that is giving them out. This is stealing. If you take one, that's fine. Unless they tell you to take them all, it is tacky to take a large number of them. They're offering them simply as a courtesy.

Limit One Per Customer specials. This is one of those gray areas. The store's intention when offering "one per customer" is generally for each customer to get the deal only once. This really means you can buy one item one time, not go back three or four times to get more. Sometimes, they say limit one per purchase. If you make more than one purchase, it may be appropriate to go back more than once. If you're not sure, ask the store manager. If your conscience is bothering you, pass it up. Sometimes stores offer special deals where they actually lose money. If they post a limit it is because they need a certain amount of sales to make up for the loss. If there's no limit, buy everything if you wish. If there's a limit, use your judgment.

You buy an item and you use it a few times and then return it because you're done with it. Stealing and lying. You probably won't tell the sales clerk you just needed to use it for a few times and even if you do, that's only OK if it is a rental store. If an item breaks, doesn't work or is not the right color, it is fine to return it. If you just needed it "for a few times" (like a dress for a special occasion) and know you won't use it again, you're taking advantage of the store if you return it.

If you eat a food item with a guarantee on the box and it tastes nasty, return it. That's why they offer a guarantee. If you eat the entire contents of the box first and return the mostly-empty box, it probably wasn't actually nasty.

If you try to pass off your 14 year old child as a 12 year old so that you only have to pay for a child's meal, you are lying and teaching your child that lying is good when it benefits you.

If you go to a restaurant where it is customary to tip, tip the customary amount (usually 15%) if the service is reasonably good. If you get good service and fail to tip, you are being mean, ungrateful and a tightwad to the server. If you can't afford the tip, go to a restaurant where it is not customary to tip (like a fast-food restaurant). If your whole family shares one entree and your kids leave a mess of ground up crackers reaching out eight feet from the table in every direction, don't just tip on the one entree. Tip on the work you create for the server.

If you find a "great deal" that you can't live without but you don't have the money in your checking account, don't write a check. Let it be the "one that got away" If you knowingly write a bad check, you are stealing and lying.

If you find a "great deal", buy it and then hide it from your husband, you're lying (unless it's his birthday present ;-). If you have to hide it, you know you're doing something wrong.

If you charge up your credit cards with frivolous things like shopping and eating out and then declare bankruptcy, you are stealing from the credit card company and from everyone who does business with that company. Bankruptcy is intended to help people who end up financially strapped because of reasons beyond their control, like catastrophic medical expenses or the death of a spouse. It is unethical to declare bankruptcy because you went on a shopping spree, because you bought something you couldn't afford when you bought it or because you decided to change careers and no longer want to pay the student loans for your old career. You signed that piece of paper when you purchased the item saying you would pay them back and you didn't. It's up to you to pay them back any (legal :-) way you can, even if it does mean feeling "deprived" for a time.

One more thing about bankruptcy: It is unethical to incur lots of debt "keeping up with the Joneses" and then go bankrupt because the debt is so large. Many people look at others and say to themselves, "Those people are the same age as me. I work hard. I deserve that too." or "our house is too small" or "our car is a real clunker so we need to buy a brand need one to "save" on repair costs (a huge myth, by the way!). If you can afford these things, by all means, buy them. If you can't afford those things, find a way to make more money or learn to be happy with what you have.

Frugal living is about making good financial decisions. There are so many things you can do to spend your money more wisely, so when you think you can get a "good deal", but it requires doing something that hurts someone else, pass it up.

Whenever you're in doubt about whether something is ethical, ask yourself if it would be OK with you if the situation were reversed and you were the person potentially coming up short. Be honest. We've all heard "Do unto others as you would have them do unto you." If you would object to others doing it to you, you better look for a better way to save.

Should We Declare Bankruptcy?

A reader writes: **My husband was a lawyer for 4 years before going to seminary and becoming a minister. Now with living on his severely reduced salary as a pastor the student loans seem like they will never be paid back. Is going bankrupt our only way out? (We still owe over $250k.)**

Tawra: I know this must be difficult for you. **This is a touchy subject for some but it's a question I get a lot.** No, going bankrupt is not the only way out.

Bankruptcy is intended to help people who end up financially strapped because of reasons beyond their control, like catastrophic medical expenses or the death of a spouse. Bankruptcy can be a good thing for emergencies, but I don't think it is ethical to claim it for "poor planning". I understand that it may feel like this situation is beyond your control, but it is actually the result of choices that your husband made. Even if he made those choices before marrying you, if you married him knowing about his debt, you accepted that responsibility with him.

I **believe that when you take out loans, even student loans, that you should not be able to claim bankruptcy on them.** You signed the note saying you would pay back the loan. The banks, credit card companies or other creditors are not responsible if you decide to change careers. If you claim bankruptcy for expenses you no longer choose to honor, it is really lying (because he promised to pay it back) and stealing (because if he stayed in law, he would have been able to repay it, rather than to make the credit card companies and their customers responsible for his decision to change his mind).

What can you do? That is a lot of money to owe and I can understand how overwhelming it must be, but it is your responsibility to pay it back. There are several options in your case:

Your husband could go back to being a lawyer, earning lawyer's pay and spending only a pastors expenses for several years, paying the balance to debt until it's paid off. This is probably the fastest and easiest way to pay it off. If your husband is serious about preaching, he could practice law and preach part time until the debt is paid.

Your husband could work part time as a lawyer and part time as a pastor.

He could continue as a full time pastor and get a part time job on the side.

You could get a job. If your kids are small and still at home then you would need to get a job during your husband's off hours so you don't have to pay day care.

Do any on the side jobs you can. Can he mow lawns? Can you do ironing or child care?

It will take a long time to pay it off but you can do it. I do think that if your husband is a pastor then he needs to pay off the debt because he is the leader of a church and it is his responsibility to set a good example to his congregation. Ministers are not perfect, but God does require a higher standard from them. I believe that if God has called your husband into the ministry, God will make a way for you to pay off the debt without having to declare bankruptcy.

Be careful about reading health books. You may die of a misprint. - Mark Twain

---

How Do We Catch Up On Debt?

Leslie from Rhode Island asks: **Where do we begin to catch up on debt when we are behind three months on every day living such as mortgage, car payments, and utilities and IRS payments?**

Jill: **It is hard to give specific answers to your question without knowing more details about all of your finances.** Here are some general suggestions about a couple of things that you mentioned. Some of these ideas may seem drastic, but if you are three months behind on everything including the IRS then you need to take a very honest and serious look at your spending habits.

In order to catch up on past due bills, you not only have to live within your income, you have to live below your income. It may be painful, but you have to figure out how to live below your income at least long enough to pay the past due bills and then to keep current on all of your bills.

If you can't keep up with your mortgage, then no matter how much you love your home you may have to sell it for something less expensive. The same goes for your cars. You could try to get by with one car. That may not be as impossible as it sounds. My son and his wife both work and often only have one car. She found she could switch to evening hours at her job for a while until they could get another car. One spouse may have to take the other to work. This may not be convenient, but declaring bankruptcy isn't really handy either. Besides, if you declared bankruptcy and still spent more than your income, you'd end up with the same problem all over again. You could also sell your cars and get less expensive/used cars with smaller payments.

Cut back on utilities as much as possible. There have been times where I couldn't run my air conditioner or I just used it when it became unbearable. Notice that I said unbearable, not uncomfortable. There's a difference. Stop watering your yard. If your lawn dies, it dies. What would you rather have? Bills that are paid, no financial stress and a dead yard or lots of debt and stress and a nice green yard? I know it seems like there is no way out but it really is doable. Start thinking about each item you buy. Do you really NEED it or do you just WANT it?

Reducing Utility Bills

Lisa writes: Hello ladies, **I was wondering if you have any wise tips on reducing our utility bills?** Our utility company just raised their rates, and we received a $300.+ electric bill this month.

Hi Lisa! Here are few tips that we use:

Keep your thermostat at 78-82 in the summer and 60-65 in the winter. For most people, this is the other way around. If you currently keep it much lower than this, try changing it over a couple months so you can get used to it. (FYI, mom keeps hers at 55 in the winter and 80 in the summer.)

Move down to the coolest part or up to the warmest part of the house. In the summer move all your beds and/or the TV down to the basement. In the winter your upstairs room maybe the warmest so move up there. Don't move everything twice a year. We have a bi-level house and immediately after moving in, we realized that even though a bi-level has bedrooms on both floors, it works better for us to live during the day all on one floor. We moved all of the sleeping arrangements downstairs, even though it meant that we used the downstairs family room for our bedroom.

In the summer, open windows in the opposite corners of the house to "draw" the air through first thing in the morning. Then close them later before the heat of the day hits.

Use fans instead of central air or even air conditioners. We don't turn on the air conditioner unless it is more than 80° F (27° C)

* Put fans in your windows backwards to draw hot air out. If you want the cooler outside air to blow across you in one room, place the fan in a window directly across the house to suck air out. Then, the cooler air will be pulled into the window where you are.

* Use attic fans to draw hot air out too. Don't underestimate how much an attic fan can help. Consider that a 125° attic next to a 78° house can raise the temperature, even with good attic insulation. It can literally drop your homes temperature's several degrees.

* Do things that require you to be up and moving around during the coolest part of the day (dusting, vacuuming, cleaning the bathroom).

* Do the things that are less physical and more stationary in front of a fan during the hotter part of the day (washing dishes, folding clothes, paying bills).

* Plan ahead for baking. In the summer when it's hot, only bake on the cooler days, ideally when you don't need the air conditioner and can keep the windows open. If you can plan ahead for the week, bake what you can in advance so that if a really hot day comes, you can avoid using the oven that day. If you fail to plan be sure to make something on the grill or in the crock-pot.

* Sometimes, you will save money on energy use by replacing an inefficient appliance. Most of the time, it will take a while for the cost of replacing the appliance to make the energy savings worth it, so don't replace something expensive just to save on your utilities unless you do the math. If you find that you need to replace an appliance soon, replace it now if you can save on energy costs since you will have to incur that cost anyway.

Our air conditioner costs us about $150 per month to cool our 1600 square foot house in the summer which is twice that of a friend with a similar sized house in town, but because of the high cost to replace one and the relatively few number of months we use it each year, we will probably wait another couple years to replace it.

* Test your power usage if you can. There is a company that makes a device that is like a plug adapter that you can use to test the power usage on any appliance that plugs into a wall. Test any appliances you can. I thought that our refrigerator was using a lot of power and then I discovered it was actually the lights.

* Don't use appliances that you can avoid using. I like line dried clothes because of the fresh smell, so I try not to use the dryer much. This helps keep the cost down and also saves money because the dryer reduces clothes' life span. For some appliances, reducing your use won't save much. Unless you own a malt shop, go ahead and use the blender as much as you usually do. ;-)

*Consider using fluorescent light bulbs if you use lot of lights. There are lots of newer style fluorescent bulbs that don't put out that nasty color and quality of light that we associate with older fluorescents. We replaced most of the light bulbs in our house all at once and our electric bill went down $40 right away. Where we live, our electric bill has gone from $100-$110 per month without the air conditioner down to $60-$70. Fluorescent bulbs can be expensive compared to incandescent, though and if you don't use your lights very often, it could be more expensive to change them than the short term savings. We keep a lot of our lights on much of the day, so it was worth it for us. Also, the fluorescents tend to last a lot longer than incandescent bulbs (about 10 years). If you decide to try fluorescents, try one or two at first. They have different color and quality characteristics and you'll want to make sure you find bulbs you like before spending the money to replace a lot of them.

Winter House

We purchased an old home in Northern New York State from two elderly sisters. Winter was fast approaching and I was concerned about the house's lack of insulation. "If they could live here all those years, so can we!" my husband confidently declared.

One November night the temperature plunged to below zero, and we woke up to find interior walls covered with frost. My husband called the sisters to ask how they had kept the house warm. After a rather brief conversation, he hung up.

"For the past 30 years," he muttered, "they've gone to Florida for the winter."

If Time is Money, Then Money is Time, Too!

When people ask me about getting out of debt, they often ask "Doesn't it take quite a bit more time to be frugal?" Of course, doing work yourself does mean you spend more time doing certain things, but it also means that you will spend a lot less time and money working to pay someone else to do it. Many people work more hours to pay someone else to do a job than it would take them to do it themselves. Of course, if you make a million dollars a year and have no manual dexterity, this article is not for you.

Here are some examples based on my own experience with a family of 4. Because your household income is probably not the same as mine, some things that make sense for me will not make sense for you. I suggest that you read my examples and consider your actual costs.

Example #1: Buying clothes- One great way to save on clothes is to go to garage sales. This seems very time consuming to many people, but it really isn't. In the summer, I usually spend 3-4 hours every 2 weeks (May - September) going to garage sales. That may seem like a lot, but if you compare that to how much time the average person spends shopping at the mall, it really isn't any longer.

Example #2: Meals- I usually average an hour and a half each day preparing and cleaning up from meals. Compare that to going out to eat: It takes the typical person 20 minutes to drive to the restaurant and 20 minutes to return home. That is 40 minutes. Then you spend 15-20 minutes ordering and waiting for your order. You are now up to one hour. If you plan an hour for eating, you are up to two hours total. Don't forget the 2-3 hours you had to work to pay for it! This assumes an income of $30,000 per year and a $40 family meal.

If you go to fast food restaurants instead, you could cut your time down to 40-50 minutes and 1-2 hours working to pay for it.

If you stay home and cook, it will cost you 15-30 minutes preparing the meal and less than $5 paying for it. I'm not saying that you should never eat out but, that if you do it regularly, it will cost you a lot more (in time and money). Is it really worth it?

Example #3: Buying a car- If you buy a new car with $500 a month payments for 5 years, you pay $30,000. Let's say you earn $30,000 per year at your job. If you assume 25% income tax, you must earn $40,000 to pay for your $30,000 car. This means that you have to work 1 year and 4 months for no other reason but to pay for that car. Is it really worth working over one year just to pay for a new car? If you decided to buy a $7500 car instead, you could afford to take a vacation from work for a year. Haven't you been saying you need more free time? (If you didn't get that, get out your calculator and do the math. This is important.)

Always consider the hidden costs, too. Would you feel more inclined to buy a security system for that $30,000 car? How much will that cost? Are the parts more expensive for the $30,000 car when it breaks down? Trust me, your new car will still break down almost as much as a used car. Ask my brother...

Be very careful when you start saying things like "Doesn't it take too much time to be frugal?" or "I can't seem to find time to be with my husband or children" or "I don't know where to start saving." Often, those are excuses that you have created to ease your guilt. If you think about it and do the math, living simply will give you more free time. If you'd rather not, you can always keep spending money and wishing you had more family time. It's your choice! But take heart- if you have read this far then you get an A+ for taking the first step and trying!

TAWRA'S FAVORITE THOUGHT OF THE DAY

Housework can't kill you, but why take the chance? - Phyllis Diller

When to Buy New or Name Brand Goods

In all my years living frugally, I have found that some things are worth buying new. Even though I often recommend shopping at garage sales and thrift stores, there are times when you don't really save anything buying an item used or cutting back on something. I have tried to figure out how to save money using cloth napkins instead of paper ones, but I just haven't been able to justify the effort when paper napkins are so inexpensive.

If the effort to make a less expensive item useful exceeds the value of the savings, it is not worth buying something used. I have put together a list of some of the things that I buy new and some of the things I try not to buy new.

Things I will buy brand new or name brand (I usually try to make sure it's on sale):

Packing tape - The Scotch brand packing tape works much better than the cheap stuff and I end up using less.

Tortillas - I buy most staple foods at Aldi, but the Aldi tortillas just don't taste as good and they stick together.

Anti Virus software - If you use a Windows computer, don't take a chance on this one. Check out the reviews to determine which one is best for you. Mike prefers PC-cillin. No matter what you use, you will want to download the updates regularly. You usually get a year of updates free. You can usually save on new software by buying it at Amazon.com.

Haircuts - Normally, I am a huge fan of the beauty college to save money on haircuts but the other day was a flop. I took my 6 and 2 year old. We were there an hour and a half! I saved $2 and a long drive across town (about $3 gas) but it wasn't worth the wait and chasing after a 2 year old for an hour. Most of that time was spent cutting their hair. I will just take Elly to my stylist (only $6 anyway) and keep giving David his haircut at home.

Disposable Diapers - With our 3rd child we used disposable diapers. With the other two, we used cloth at home and disposables when we went out. I tried the cheap disposable diapers but they leak every time. I found that Luv's are cheaper than Pampers but still work. I did get some really cheap diapers free. I used those for during the day when I changed him more often, but never a night.

Major appliances - Most new appliances are so energy efficient, that unless you know for sure it's a year or less old, buy a new one. Do your homework. Spend the $5.95 for a one month subscription to Consumer Reports Online and study it carefully. It is worth buying a specific brand if it is significantly more likely to last.

Shoes - Mike and I have foot problems and need good shoes. We can't find used shoes that aren't completely worn out, so we buy new shoes (but always on sale). We buy used shoes for the kids as much as possible, but with our 8 year old it's getting harder. Most boys shoes are just worn out because boys tear them up before they outgrow them.

AAA roadside assistance - For a reasonable annual subscription, you can have someone make minor repairs or tow your car if you have car trouble. It's worth it not to worry about breaking down and trying to get someone to help you. We've used this to get flat tires fixed, to have a locksmith replace the ignition switch on our pickup and to tow vehicles to the shop while we were traveling.

Kids Blow up Swimming Pools - Most used ones have holes so it's not worth the risk.

Electronics - Unless you know how to fix them or unless you know they are working, it's not worth the chance. If possible, do some research before buying electronics as the price does not necessarily reflect the quality.

Anything that sells new for under $10 - Don't buy something that's used that "needs a little work" if you only save $5. Usually "a little work" ends up being a lot of work and it's not worth the hour or two (or longer) to fix it.

Canning - I don't recommend canning if your purpose is to save money. By the time you buy the fruit or vegetables and the sugar and then spend hours canning, it's not worth it unless you get most of the ingredients for free. If you do your own canning because you like to grow your own organic produce, then you have other reasons besides the financial for doing it and you can decide whether or not it is worth it for you to do it.

Things I will try not to pay full price for:

Except for the things I listed above, I usually try to buy as many things as possible used or at a substantial discount. I buy most of our food staples at Aldi, a small discount warehouse grocery store.

Cars - Much of the price of a new car is based on the "wow" value of having a new car. When a person buys a new car, the value of the car immediately drops to less than the amount that the buyer owes on the loan when the buyer drives it off the car lot. If you buy a used car, you will save a lot of money. If possible, save your money before you need a car and buy it with cash.

Shop around for one that has low miles compared to the other cars in your price range. If you look at a lot of cars, you can usually find a deal that will surprise you. If you don't know anything about cars, find a friend who does and bring that friend with you. If you find a car you like, you can also ask your mechanic to look at it for you for a reasonable fee. It is well worth having it checked out of you're not sure.

Clothes - I have noticed a difference when I buy Eddie Bauer, Van Heusen and other more expensive clothes. The colors are richer. They don't fade as bad and they last longer than Wal-mart clothes. I still wouldn't buy them new unless they were dirt cheap. I get them at the thrift store "like new" for less than $3 for dress shirts and .99 for T-shirts.

Most Furniture - I have young children and I don't generally buy new furniture because I know that it will inevitably get scratched/stained/destroyed before its time. I buy most furniture at garage sales. I'm pretty selective so that I get good quality items that match my decor.

Couch - When you have kids, why buy a new one? Kids are especially hard on couches. Unless it has a print that really hides stains, just get a used one until they are older or out of the house. I spent $90 on the one we have now. I saved over $500 and can sell it for at least $50, probably more, when I'm done with it. If you have already purchased an expensive couch then a slipcover is worth the price with kids!

Toys and almost everything for kids and babies - Until they get to be a certain age, kids don't know whether something is new or not. Even after they are 8 or so, you can get by with buying used items and re-packing them tastefully. For example, I bought a super sized package of Knex (a construction toy with lots of little pieces) and put it in a large plastic container. I bought the Knex for $10, but they would have cost more than $100 new. If you buy used and dress it up, you haven't lost as much if they don't play with it.

Camping Equipment - For items like tents, camp stoves and lanterns, most people don't use them enough to justify the cost of buying them new. If we need something, we usually buy it at a garage sale from the people who bought it new and almost never used it. Like exercise equipment, there is a lot of it out there so you can always get a good deal.

Books - Books are so expensive when you buy them new off the shelf. Our library sells used books. You can also get them at used bookstores, thrift stores and garage sales. If you must have the latest title now (a diet book, self help book or something you saw on Oprah :-), there are ways to save quite a bit. Try Half.com, E-bay or Amazon.com. For young kids, you can definitely find it much less used!

These are some of my suggestions based on things that I buy. You may find that it is worth it for you to buy something new that I buy used. It's different for everyone. The thing to remember is that for each item you buy, there is a cost and a benefit. Try to get the greatest benefit for the lowest cost.

Imagine if every Thursday your shoes exploded if you tied them the usual way.

This happens to us all the time with computers, but nobody thinks of complaining. - Jeff Raskin

---

When Should You Buy A Newer Car?

Michael from Wilmington, NC asks: **When should you get rid of an old car that is paid for and buy a newer one** that would hopefully have less maintenance cost. I am assuming the new car would be paid for outright without credit expenses.

That is a good question. **We recommend buying cars outright with no credit debt and then driving them until they die completely** or until it is no longer practical to keep them. When we buy cars, we like to pay cash and we generally pay $2000 to $6000 for the newest low mileage used car when can find. Our last two "new" cars were a 1991 Buick Skylark we bought in 1998 with 50,000 miles for $2500 and a 2000 Ford Taurus station wagon with 59,000 miles we bought in 2004 for $6000. We paid more for the Taurus because it was only four years old, it was in really good shape and we thought it was worth paying a little more for the car Tawra and the kids would be using regularly. (We also hoped it would last a little longer than some of our previous buys).

When we buy a used car, we usually choose well enough that it needs very few repairs in the first year or two. Generally, we expect to pay regular maintenance costs (new tires, oil changes, brake pads, etc.) no matter what car we drive, so we usually don't count those expenses as "repairs". We will continue to drive the car, making regular repairs until we begin to get the sense that its life span is coming to an end. When we do have to make repairs on a car, we consider it reasonable to spend several hundred dollars a couple times a year to keep it going. This might include replacing a water pump, doing major brake work or general engine work.

Usually, a catastrophic repair (like a new transmission or a new engine) is the death nail for one of our cars since our purchase price for a replacement is usually low. Occasionally, we will fix a catastrophic repair if the car rarely needs work and if we have not had the car very long. Here's an example where we did that:

Once we received a used car as a gift from family after I crashed a car on an icy road. Two weeks later, the transmission failed. Since the car was new to us, didn't cost us anything and seemed to be OK otherwise, we went ahead and spent $2000 to fix the transmission.

Most of the time, a car needs only occasional repairs, but over time, the frequency of repairs increases. When it seems that the number of repairs is on the rise, we try to figure out whether or not we think it is a trend. If so, we think of the car as "on its way out" and stop making unnecessary repairs. If we have decided that a car is "on its way out" and it requires a single repair over $500, we will usually consider it dead and replace it. If the car that is a short timer needs several lesser repairs over several months that begin to add up to a lot of money, we will usually get rid of it and get something else.

We have a 1991 Buick Skylark that was a good car for a long time. We originally bought it for $2500 in 1998 when it had 50,000 miles on it. Until 2004, it needed only occasional repairs, so we didn't feel too bad if we had to put $300 into it from time to time. In 2004, the repairs seemed to come more frequently and we began to think that the car would need to be replaced soon.

We still continued to do regular maintenance, but avoided spending a lot of money on repairs that were not critical. We got a crack in the windshield that was a little bit annoying, but since it was only around the edges and Kansas law did not require us to replace it, we decided not to repair it at the time. Again, we were pretty sure the car was on its way down hill. The heater started to occasionally smell like anti freeze which made me think the heater core was going to fail in a year or two.

We started to notice that the paint was peeling from the rear fenders, but because we didn't think the car was going to last a long time, we decided not to re-paint the car. We still made some regular repairs, but eventually, the car had a brake failure that was difficult to put a price on. We had already spend $500 in the previous 3 months for regular repairs above general maintenance and it appeared that the brake problem could cost another $300-$400.

At this point, we decided that the white car had exceeded its useful life, since we would have spent $900 in just a few months if we repaired it and we would still have had a car with a cracked windshield, a dying heater core, peeling paint and other problems that we had not yet discovered.

You will want to consider where your car is in it's useable life. If you want to keep your expenses low, always remember that a car's basic purpose is to get you from place to place reliably. You can keep more of your money if you're not driving the car to impress other people. We usually try to keep the cars looking presentable, but we normally go for clean "plain Jane" cars that run well. All major systems should work well. We live in Kansas, where the temperatures are often over the 100° mark in the summer, so we think that Air Conditioning is a must. When we lived in Colorado, we considered it more of an "option".

When it is clear that a car no longer fulfills it's basic purpose: to get you from place to place reliably within a reasonable budget, it's time to get another one.

You are wise in considering a newer "used" car when you replace an older car. Usually, you get the best buy on a car that is new enough to need few repairs, but old enough to be relatively inexpensive. You have to shop around to make sure that you find a good used car with no signs of trouble and it is wise to have a mechanic check it out of you don't know much about cars.

We try to stick to cars with 60,000 miles or less that appear to have been well maintained and cost between $2000 and $6000.

For Readers considering buying "New":

Brand new cars cost more than they are actually worth, so it's best to let someone else take the financial hit of being the first buyer of a car. Some people buy brand new cars expecting to "save" on maintenance costs and repairs, but all cars require occasional maintenance and repairs and parts for new cars tend to be more expensive.

The "white car" cost us $2500. We drove it for 8 years, so it cost us $312.50 per year. We averaged $300 per year for repairs, so our total cost for the car was $612.50 per year. That's PER YEAR, NOT PER MONTH. A similar car purchased new costs $446 per month. That is $5352 per year or $26,760 after five years of payments. Buying used, we saved $4852 per year or $24,260 for the entire cost of the car.

If you still think the new car is worth it, don't forget that the new car will cost you more in insurance and registration fees and after two years, you will probably be putting money into repairs on top of your monthly payment. It's something to think about.

Should We Sell Our Fancy House and Buy A More Modest One?

Rebejay from Vancouver, Washington asks: **Is it better to sell the fancy house, pay off all debt and rent until we can purchase a more affordable modest home?** We may have enough equity to accomplish it all and not rent. We are tired of the rat race and want to send our kids to a Christian School. We both work and can make the debt payments - just tired of being a slave to them. I want to simplify. We want to pay it all off and have the burden lifted. Also worried about housing market crashing...

Tawra: **I would say go for a modest house and get out of debt.** Even though our culture tells us we should have everything, there is no reason that we need all of the "stuff" that the popular culture says we should have. The reason they say we need the "stuff" is supposed to be to make us happier. Clearly, it doesn't sound like the fancy house is making you happier, so sell it, and the sooner the better. I would do everything possible to sell it and buy the modest one right away. We have not had good experiences renting and unless you plan to live in the rental for a number of years, renting would mean that you would have to deal with moving twice in a short time period which is exhausting and costly. Once you sell the fancy house, you shouldn't have a problem getting a mortgage on a more modest one unless you lose big money selling the fancy one or unless your credit has been negatively impacted since you got the mortgage on the first one.

Once you get the more modest home, try to pay the same amount you're currently paying for your house, allocating the difference in your old payment and your new payment to the principal. If your fancy house costs $1500 per month and your new house costs $1000 per month, pay the extra $500 to principal on the modest house. Make sure you indicate on your mortgage payment coupon that you want the balance to go to principal so that you pay it off faster. You'd be surprised how quickly you can pay it off over-paying the principal and since you can make your current payments, you can keep paying the same amount and eliminate your debt completely.

I would do everything possible to get TOTALLY out of debt. Most people don't consider a mortgage a debt, but it is. Once it is paid off, you will be able to use all of the money that you currently use for housing for something else, like the Christian School you mentioned. Not only that, one day, you will want to work less. Hopefully, you will not become disabled, but it does happen and it would be easier to have the flexibility of having no debt.

Regarding the housing market, it is a reasonable concern, but in most (but not all) areas the values will increase eventually even if they go down for a few years. Still, if you pay off your house completely, you won't have to devote time to thinking about it. Go with your instinct!

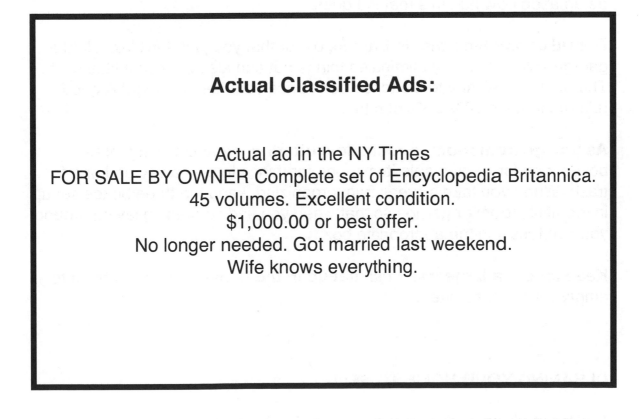

Actual Classified Ads:

Actual ad in the NY Times
FOR SALE BY OWNER Complete set of Encyclopedia Britannica.
45 volumes. Excellent condition.
$1,000.00 or best offer.
No longer needed. Got married last weekend.
Wife knows everything.

Get The Most Money
Selling Your House

A clean neat house can add an additional $5,000- $10,000 to your asking price. Using this method we sold our house in 10 days.

As soon as you find out that you are moving, start getting rid of things you don't need or use any more. It is ridiculous to move things that are never used to another house. They will merely clutter your space as they did before. Get rid of all of it!!!

To begin de-cluttering, start with one room or one cabinet at a time. Packing while carrying out your usual routine may make it easier. For example, pack the bathroom cabinet while the kids are in the tub or de-clutter a kitchen drawer while you are waiting for something to boil. You will be amazed how fast this method goes.

Get rid of anything that is broken, old or that you just don't like. Hold a garage sale, it not only eliminates things but can also provide a little cash. The goal is to eliminate clutter so don't price your items to high! A good rule of thumb is 10%-25% of retail.

As you go from room to room de-cluttering, organize using three boxes: one for garage sale items, one for things to give away and one for trash. When you take a break from organizing, keep the three boxes set up in the utility room or garage so that when you find something laying around you can toss it in the appropriate box.

Keep an extra large trash can set up in the house. You won't have to empty the trash as often.

CLEANING YOUR HOME TO SELL

Clutter is visually disturbing to potential buyers.
On of the biggest reasons houses don't sell is they are cluttered and/or dirty.

When you are trying to sell your house and you will be showing it to potential buyers, pack up things that you only use occasionally. Stack all your packed boxes in the garage or the corner of a room. This is NOT the time to make your house comfortable for you, but attractive to sell.

After you have de-cluttered, it is time to DEEP CLEAN.

KITCHEN - Clean the sink, stove and refrigerator. Don't forget to clean the fronts of your cabinets. Wipe fingerprints off of everything, including walls and light switch plates. Remove as much as you can from the counter tops. Make sure that the space under your kitchen sink is clean because everyone always checks the plumbing under the sink. Sweep, mop the floor and empty the trash.

BEDROOMS - Make beds, pick up clothes, clear off dressers, end tables and other furniture. Dust, vacuum and make sure closets are uncluttered, neat and clean.

BATHROOM - Put away (meaning in a box or drawer out of sight) all bathroom items including makeup, shampoos, baby toys and toiletries. Clean the sink, tub and toilet. One trick I learned while cleaning houses professionally was to take a soft cloth and dry everything well, to prevent water spots. It is especially important to shine the metal fixtures. Clean under the sink, empty the trash and wipe off light switch plates. Mop the floor. As in the kitchen, the less clutter you have, the better. Keep one nice set of towels handy that you can put out when you are showing the house.

LIVING ROOM - Remove all unnecessary items that are laying around on the furniture including toys, magazines and newspapers. Remove all pictures and accessories that are not adding to the decor of the room, either pack them or garage sale them. Dust (don't forget to dust the pictures on the walls) and vacuum.

GARAGE - Don't overlook the garage! Make sure things are neatly placed and sweep the floor. Place all items in boxes if you can. Neatly stacked boxes give a better impression than piles of stuff.

Continue going through each room using the same basic ideas.

If your carpets are dirty be sure to either rent a carpet cleaner or have them professionally cleaned. Seeing all kinds of carpet stains from kids is a big turn off to potential buyers.

SHOWING YOUR HOUSE

Keep a basket in each room so that you can quickly throw things in it when you have to show your home. This is particularly useful if you have children and you usually have toys on the floor. Hide the basket with a nice blanket.

Don't leave open trash cans sitting around.

Turn lights on in every room including the garage. This will make the house show better.

In a potpourri pot or pan, simmer some cinnamon with either or all of the following: ginger, nutmeg, or cloves. It is best to stay away from strong scented candles with berry, apple, peach or other similar smells because some people find these scents overpowering and unpleasant. Most people do however like the smell of cinnamon.

IF YOUR HOUSE IS VACANT

If you are leaving your home and it will be shown vacant, here are a couple of ideas to help make it show better.

Take a few small terra cotta pots and fill with 2 or 3 stems of silk geraniums. (Geraniums aren't necessarily my favorite flower but the bright red color works great for this purpose). Place them in several different corners of the house. A couple on the kitchen counter, one on the back of the toilet, or counter in the bathroom, a corner of the living room or on the mantle of the fireplace.

Place a bouquet of real looking silk flowers and small bowl of potpourri in your entryway for people to see when they first walk in. First impressions are very important. Don't get carried away by making the house look like a florist shop. It takes just a couple of splashes of color here and there to really warm up an empty house.

Moving On A Dime
Save Money, Save Time, Save Your Sanity!

ORDER IN WHICH TO START PACKING

Start with things you don't use every day.

* **Memories -** Grandma's dishes, quilts, old books, Bibles, childhood toys and photos

* **Garage items -** Christmas and Holiday decorations, camping equipment and things in storage

* **Things stored in closets** that aren't used often and out of season clothes

* **Knick-knacks, pictures, mirrors and wall hangings**

* **Seasonal** dishes, canning equipment, roasting pans, good china, good silverware, large serving platters

* **Unnecessary CD's, DVD's and video tapes.**

* **Sewing room and craft items.**

* **Home office -** Pack as much as possible except bills that need to be paid. Leave office boxes open and tape them closed at the last minute before moving just in case you need something out of them.

* **Children's toys and games -** Pack most of the toys they don't play with regularly.

* **One week before moving,** pack all unnecessary kitchen items, clothes and linens (except what you need for one week).

PAIN FREE PACKING

Don't leave empty spaces. Here are some examples of how you might use all available space:

* **I fill my china cabinet with light weight soft things** like stuffed animals, balls of yarn, quilts, artificial flowers and greenery.

* **If you will be moving your refrigerator** or washer or dryer, fill it with pillows, wicker baskets or plastic items from the kitchen.

* **Fill clothes hampers with bathroom items.** If you have a lamp that needs special protection, wrap it carefully in towels and place it in a clothes hamper.

* **Fill up even small items like plastic pitchers** with kitchen utensils or kitchen knick-knacks.

* **I clean out a large outside trash can** and use it to pack my hoses, small pots and gardening tools. If I'm not sure if I should keep something, I allow myself to take it if I can fit it in that one trash can. My son-in-law says it is one step closer to the curb that way. ;-)

* **Don't pack glass,** porcelain or ceramic containers with loose items in them that could break them. Canning jars filled with marbles or baby food jars filled with nuts and bolts are recipes for disaster.

* **Pack heavy things such as books in small boxes.**

* **Don't pack things like photos,** videotapes, cd's, candles, plants or pets (especially pets!!!) where heat or cold can get to them. Don't think any of those things will be safe and protected in a car or truck overnight. If it gets cold, they will freeze. Also plants left in a hot car will not be safe because the heat will kill them. When transporting plants in a car, protect them from direct sunlight with a covering of newspaper because the sun will fry houseplants.

* **Pack kids' rooms last.** They need the security of having their room the same for as long as possible. Be sure to put their favorite items in the car such a blanket, stuffed animal or books.

How to Have a Garage Sale

Your objective is to make money while getting rid of stuff in your house. The spring is the best time to have a garage sale. After a long winter people are ready to get out and find some good deals. Here are some tips to make the most of your garage sale:

Have as many signs as possible. Put one on every major corner, on the corner to house and any needed in between. If it is more than 1/2 mile from the corner to your house put some signs in between. You really can't make enough signs.

*Make your signs large!!** At least 12 inches but 18-24 is much better.

*Use contrasting colors.** Black and white are best but other colors such as light colored paper with black ink will work well. A black permanent marker works best.

*Be sure to put your address AND an arrow** pointing the direction to your house.

*Make all your signs out of the same material.** For example, make all of them out of cardboard with white painting. That way people will know it's your garage sale and know which signs to follow.

*Check with your city or town and find out if they have any particular rules for garage sales.** Our city requires a permit that costs $1.50 per day. When we purchase the permit, they give us a list of rules telling us things like not to nail signs on telephone poles.

Check to see if any of your local papers or thrifty papers have free garage sale ads. Put one in if they do.

Clean out everything you can so you can have as large as sale as possible.

*If you don't have enough stuff to make a big enough sale,** then ask friends, family or neighbors to have one with you.

*Give all of your neighbors a flyer telling them when you are having a sale and ask if they would like to have one also. The more sales that there are in one area, the more people will come to your sale.

Price you stuff LOW. There is nothing more frustrating than going to a garage sale and finding items for prices equal to or higher than the same items brand new on clearance, even if it is "Baby Gap". Name brands can let you get by with a little higher price.

I recommend pricing really nice kids clothes no higher than $1 each and clothes that have stains or are not name brand at .50 or less. Socks and underwear shouldn't be higher than .10 each.

You may think that these prices are too low but please remember than you are getting rid of stuff!! You don't want to bring it back into the house and store it for a few more years. If you are not selling to get rid of things, you will keep most of what you put out. You will also get a lot more sales if your prices are reasonable which means more in the long run. If you sell 15 $1 items or you sell 200 @ .25 each ($50 total) you will make much more if you sell the less expensive items. A good rule of thumb is to price items a maximum of 10% retail price.

By the way, people who go to yard sales really don't care if it's brand new in the box and you paid $80 for it so you "must" get $50 for it. It has been sitting in your house for who knows how long so you aren't getting your money's worth anyway. Price it for $5 and get rid of it!

Expect people to ask you to come down on the price. If you feel your prices are very reasonable then don't come down, but remember you are trying to get rid of stuff so don't put too high a value on it. If someone asks you to come down on a price and you aren't ready to come down at that point ask for their name and number and tell them you will call them later if it hasn't sold and you are ready to sell it to them at that price.

Ten Garage Sale Shortcuts

1. There are two kinds of garage sales – the ones where people want to make money and the ones where people want to get rid of stuff. The object is to find the ones where people want to get rid of stuff.

2. Get a map and newspaper and map out your route. Photocopying a map from a phone book or printing one from the web works great. Using this method, you can easily visit 25 sales an hour. If you're a beginner you might hit neighborhoods you are familiar with first.

3. If at all possible leave the kids at home. If you must take them use a baby backpack or an umbrella stroller to make it easier. Give older children 25 or 50 cents and let them see what good deals they can get. Kids love picking out gifts for grandparents, siblings, parents and other family and bargain hunting helps them learn about money. Bring snacks (animal crackers, cereals, crackers in plastic bag works well) and cold water for everyone and plan ahead for potty breaks. If you have children with you, it's best only to plan on hitting about five sales until you see how they do.

4. Wear cool, comfortable clothes. Bring lots of change and one dollar bills. Put your money in your pockets so you don't have to worry about carrying your purse. Also bring a tote bag in which to carry your finds as you walk.

5. When you find something you're not sure you want, pick it up and carry it around while you continue looking. Otherwise someone else may take it while you're trying to decide.

6. Always ask politely if they will come down on the price. Most of the time they will. Every once in a while some things are so reasonable that I do not feel right asking for less. Finding women's sweater's at $1.00 each isn't bad, but I still ask if they will take 50 or 75 cents. If I find a name brand sweater in perfect shape for 25 cents, I don't ask for less.

7. If there is something you really want, but the seller is asking more than you want to pay, offer them a lower price. If they say no, leave your name and number and ask them to consider selling it to you at your price if they still have it at the end of the day.

8. Always check items well for hard to see tears, stains, or breakage. Remember it is a garage sale so everything won't be perfect.

9. It is best to go early, but don't panic if you can't. Sometimes you get the best buys after lunch when sellers are tired and don't want to have to drag everything back into the house. It's great to go on the last day of a sale because most sellers will almost pay you to take things so they don't have to keep them.

10. If you don't have success in one part of town, try somewhere else the next time. Sometimes the best garage sale neighborhoods are the ones you don't expect.

Don't be embarrassed about buying at garage sales. Some of the wealthiest women in the world love garage sales - Martha Stewart and Oprah are among them! When you're done, go home, put up your feet and have a nice glass of ice cold lemonade. Grab the phone and call someone who will share the excitement and appreciate your good buys. Garage sales are like old fishing stories. Die-hards always brag about the one that got away!

Additional Hints From a Reader:

Thanks for the article, Tawra and Jill.

I wanted to share with you that it also pays to carry along a box (or boxes) with paper for wrapping if you like to buy glassware or delicate items.

We did estate sale purchasing (and some garage sale shopping) for vintage items for our country store. Taking the time to wrap the delicate items and put them into boxes, well paid for the time (as we quickly learned when some things didn't make it home unbroken!).

By going shopping together one could drive on to the next sale while the other wrapped those special items! It was great team work.

And speaking of children going, our oldest daughter does Ebay selling and all of the 6 children are trained into what to look for value and they each scout out possibilities in different areas while Mom looks also!

The children also take some of their finds and have made very good money selling them on Ebay--sometimes $50-$100 profit!

The grandkids run from 4 to 16. The 4 year old is pretty much an expert into Pooh and Bob the Builder though! If the sale has any of those products, he isn't much help with the other items! :-)   The family of 8 is able to stay completely wardrobed from garage sales (and a few thrift stores) solely--from church clothes to farm clothes!

Thanks for the articles you both write.

--Linda

Why Ask Why?

How come you never hear father-in-law jokes?

Why do they use sterilized needles for death by lethal injection?

Why doesn't Tarzan have a beard?

And my FAVORITE....

The statistics on sanity are that one out of every four persons is suffering from some sort of mental illness. Think of your three best friends -- if they're okay, then it's you.

It's all Perspective

by Ami DePierro

Am I cheap for using the library? I prefer to think that I am spending quality time with my kids (story time) and (hopefully) instilling a love of reading into them. I also prefer to view reading as an intellectual pursuit and not cheap entertainment.

Am I cheap for reusing baggies. No, I am caring about my environment.

Is my house decorated with yard sale junk? No it is done with "antiques and collectibles"

Am I cheap for giving homemade gifts. No, I care enough about the person to spend a little time and put some effort in their gift.

Am I cheap for not going out to eat at a restaurant with hubby or am I a romantic for packing a picnic and going to the park to watch the sunset instead?

Am I cheap for wearing the same pair of jeans for the last 10 years or am I just good at watching my weight?

Am I cheap for sharing a shower with hubby or am I a sex goddess? He picks number two.

Am I cheap for reusing things and refinishing furniture. I prefer to think I am creative and crafty.

Am I cheap because I go to yard sales. NO I am a voyeur who gets a kick out of seeing other people's junk and if I happened to find a good deal while browsing at an "estate sale" so be it.

Am I cheap when I demand that the $.08 that I was overcharged be refunded. No I am a consumer rights activist.

It's all how you look at it!

My Conversion Story
How I Went From Spendthrift to Tightwad in Four Short Years
By Michael Kellam

Dear Readers, One question people often ask is **"How do I stop spending money when my bills are out of control."** They don't usually say it up front but if I ask, they are usually quick to admit that they just don't want to give up the things they want. My husband Mike wrote about how he changed his thinking when confronted with this situation. Hopefully, his story will give you some measure of inspiration in your situation.

Tawra

Being frugal is a way of life. It does not mean giving up everything that you have or want, but it does mean that you have to be more selective about which things that you buy. When you have control over your finances, you will not be a slave to your debt or your job and you will gain the freedom to live your life the way you choose. Traveling the road to frugality can be a choice or a necessity. For us, it was a necessity. Here is my story.

I have made a 180 degree change in the way I think about money. After college, I lived in my parents house while working the grocery store job I had worked since high school. I made $1300 a month at a time when I had no bills. I spent money to make myself feel good, eating out daily, going to movies frequently and buying a whole host of consumer items each of which only held my interest a few days. My frivolous spending was so out of control that this was not enough play money and I quickly spent $4000 that my grandmother had saved for me since I was a baby. Still, I did not learn and began charging my deficit on credit cards.

My first wake up call was when I was declined additional credit after maxing out all of my credit cards. When I moved out of my parents' house, I had a very difficult time managing my money. I was able to pay only the minimum payments on my credit cards and resented the evil credit card companies who had done this to me, not admitting that I was the problem.

When I got married in 1994, my wife and I disagreed about money. I thought it was everyone's "right" to have some money to play with, but she had lived most of her life with no money and wanted to eliminate every bit of unnecessary spending so that we could pay off debt. As we slowly paid down some of the debt, I began believing more that Tawra's methods could improve our financial situation, but I was still unhappy about giving up the fun stuff.

In 1996, we moved to Idaho for a job that fell through when we arrived. We had no money, I had no job and we were in a small town a long way from a city. In spite of no money we were determined not to charge anything. We gave a lot of thought to what items were needs and which were wants. We did not have a lot of basic household items that most people take for granted. We did not have a refrigerator or freezer. It was winter in Idaho so we stored our cold items outside in a utility shed. One day, some cats got into our shed and tried to eat our last two pounds of round steak, leaving teeth marks in the frozen meat. We anguished over whether we should throw away the meat, but since we could not afford to get rid of it, we cut off the bite marks and cooked it anyway. This was the beginning of my turnaround.

I got a job and we bought a small and very inexpensive house. We cut our own wood for heat, planted gardens and slowly worked to pay off the debt. We scavenged a lot of garden material (pots, potting soil, bricks, plants, etc.), used building supplies and furniture from dumpsters outside of our town. We even made some money selling dumpster finds at garage sales. Along the way, we had two children and incurred some unexpected medical bills. Still, we were able to pay off $20,000 in debt in the first 5 years we were in Idaho while averaging $22,000 per year.

There was one more incident that made me realize how completely I had turned my thinking around. Tawra's family gives money at holidays instead of gifts sometimes. Since we had cut all of our unnecessary expenses, this money was all we had to buy ourselves "fun" stuff. At first, I bought myself a few CD's and some other items that I again lost interest in quickly. I decided to save for a bigger and better item, but after saving the money, I was unable to bring myself to spend it. I asked myself "Do I really need this?" and "What if something better comes along?" I have since joked with Tawra and her mom that they ruined me since now I can't even bring myself to spend the fun money!

When I wrote this, **I earned $1700 a month which we use to support our family of four (Tawra, myself and two pre-schoolers).** We now laugh at the fact that I came from a mindset of being unable to make it with no bills and a $1300 a month income to being able to support a family of four on $1700 a month. Take heart anguishing spendthrifts! It is possible to change. **It takes a little time and determination, but it is definitely worth the effort.**

MISDIRECTED!

Consider the case of the Illinois man who left the snow-filled streets of Chicago for a vacation in Florida. His wife was on a business trip and was planning to meet him there the next day.

When he reached his hotel, he decided to send his wife a quick e-mail. Unable to find the scrap of paper on which he had written her e-mail address, he did his best to type it in from memory. Unfortunately, he missed one letter and his note was directed instead to an elderly preacher's wife, whose husband had passed away only the day before. When the grieving widow checked her e-mail she took at look at the monitor, let out a piercing scream, and fell to the floor in a dead faint.

At the sound, her family rushed into the room and saw this note on the screen: Dearest Wife, Just got checked in. Everything prepared for your arrival tomorrow. P.S. Sure is hot down here!

Don't Buy In!

By Michael Kellam

Did you know you need a new cell phone? Did you know your car is trash? Did you know you're not pretty enough, you're overweight, you wear outdated clothes, you need to eat healthier and you need two large pizzas? If you didn't know that, brace yourself because that's just the beginning of your troubles -- or so say the messages bombarding virtually every one of us every day.

Do you realize how much advertising you are subjected to each day? There are ads on television, ads on the radio, ads on the Internet, ads in the paper, in magazines, along the side of the road and on other vehicles. There are ads in virtually every business you walk into each day and there are ads all over your house. The next time you go to Wal-Mart, pause at the front door and take a careful inventory of all the advertising you are exposed to in that one location. There are hundreds, possibly thousands of print ads competing for your attention there. Wal-Mart radio plays a constant barrage of advertising trying to influence you to buy something. Many of the items available for purchase practically cry out to you to purchase them through advertising on the packaging. Even if you are the queen of frugality, you cannot help but be influenced by this daily barrage of advertising.

What many people don't know is that the basic purpose of advertising is to persuade you to buy something you didn't know you needed before you saw the ad. The message isn't usually, "Hey, if you have a few extra dollars, you might enjoy this product." The typical advertising message you hear really says something more like "Even though you never needed this product before, your friends and family will reject you, you will encounter daily torment, you will discover that you have no value as a human being and that you will probably die if you don't buy this product right away!"

As competition for your attention gets more and more fierce, you get bombarded with more and more types of ads and more intense ads. It is like standing in the middle of a crowded group of people where each one is yelling at you trying to get you to pay attention to him. As time goes on, the whole group begins yelling louder and louder because each person is trying to out-shout the rest of the group.

Have you noticed an increased intensity in advertising during your life? I remember when grocery companies first used advertising on the back of register receipts. Then, one day, the store added mini-billboards to all of their shopping carts. Then they added advertising to the shopping basket carrels in the parking lot. At the time, those seemed like innovative ideas. Now, they just get lost in the "muck" of advertising. Recently, I was filling up my car with gas in Colorado and discovered that since I was last there, the gas station added video screens at the gas pump so that they could hit customers with a fresh barrage of advertising during one of those rare moments of near silence that many of us ever get. I heard today that a company is now trying to sell grocery stores on the idea of advertising actually printed on the conveyor belts where you set your groceries while you wait your turn in line. I don't know who will be the first company to actually believe that that will be an effective way to make sales in a spot where customers are already overwhelmed with so many competing messages. At our grocery store, we are already assaulted with messages from tabloids and magazines with headlines designed to suck us in with the shock value. There are ads on the little dividers we put between our groceries and those of the next person in line. Is it really necessary to add yet another layer of mind "noise" to our lives?

I already mentioned that the purpose of advertising is to persuade you to buy something you have never needed before. Did you know that the main purpose of the media is to sell advertising so you have more urgency to buy something you have never needed before? Oh, you thought that the purpose of television was to entertain and inform you? Think again! Television shows are only produced to act as the "sugar" to get you to take the bad tasting medicine. You may wonder how I came to think this way. I have a four year communications degree, having majored in Radio, Television and Film. The principle that television and radio shows exist as a means to get people to watch ads was a major concept in the Radio, Television and Film program.

TV ads are, as a whole louder than ever, often using fast paced tense music to make you feel like there is an urgent reason you need to watch this commercial. Even though there are laws designed to prevent television broadcasters from playing commercials louder than shows, commercial producers know how to mix the audio in such a way that the

41

commercial sounds louder without appearing louder to the broadcast equipment. Have you ever noticed that many commercials have the sound of a telephone near the beginning, even if a phone doesn't play any part in the "story" of the ad? That's because production companies know that the sound of a phone ringing will cause most people to unconsciously respond with urgency to the ringing of a telephone.

Even magazines are in business to sell you advertising. Oh I'm not talking about the tabloids with "too good to be true" advertising that is so obvious to most of us. I'm talking about the magazine where you read a story about some new gizmo that the "reviewer" in the magazine seems to think is the greatest thing out there. Many of the magazine articles that appear to be written by impartial reporters singing the graces of various products are actually advertisements, commissioned by the companies that sell those products, written by advertising agencies and provided to the magazines as "stories" designed to make you think that some regular Joe out there liked the product so much he just had to recommend it to you.

If you still haven't heard enough, think about the news. When you watch, listen to or read the news, do you ever ask yourself whether or not the information that you are getting is true? Most people never question the news. If you're in your mid 30s like I am, you have probably heard that news is impartial, that reporters are supposed to report the news without interjecting their own opinions. That's what the editorial pages are for, right? Though this would be a great way for the news to work, it is not the reality.

Recently, there was a story on the news at one of the major stations here in Wichita called "Family Fears Africanized Bees Could Be In Kansas". The story told of a family in Southern Kansas that thought a hive of bees in their back yard might be killer bees. According to the news report, the lady that was stung had been close to the bees before and had never been stung until the date of the story. Because the lady got stung, the couple assumed that they "may" be killer bees. The news report implied that this was a reason for concern for people in Kansas with this new threat. The reporter did not put an expert on camera attesting to the likelihood that they were killer bees. There was nothing in the story to suggest that the bees were killer bees except that someone got stung. Wow, does that mean every time I've ever been stung by a bee that it was a dreaded "Killer" bee?

Come to think of it, why are killer bees called "killer"? When we lived in Texas, the news talked about "killer" bees coming to Texas. Now, more than a decade after the killer bees arrived there, I wonder why there aren't thousands of people falling victim to this deadly plague. Considering how few people die from killer bee stings, I wonder why the media doesn't do more stories about being killed by meteors falling from the sky. Still, there are many people who get stressed out seeing stories like this on the news for no good reason.

I say all this to make the point that news operations make their money from advertising and in order to keep you watching, newscasters have realized that it is easiest to keep you watching when you are constantly afraid of what will happen if you don't see the news today. Just like with advertisers, people in the news business are trying to sell you something. Because of this fact, you only see the news that is likely to make you want to keep watching and to tune in for every newscast. This means that you get a distorted view of the real world because of "selective coverage" that tends to portray the world as a place with dangers waiting to attack you with every decision you make in life. Also, because many reporters are young with very little practical life experience and because reporters have only a few hours to develop the story, broadcast news is full of errors.

The bee story is a great example because many people hear a story on the news and begin assimilating the information as if it is factual. Even if you are a reasonable person, repeatedly hearing someone profess ridiculous things can make you question what you believe. Joseph Goebbels, author of the Nazi propaganda campaign against the Jews said that "if you tell a lie often enough, it eventually becomes accepted as the truth."

There are all kinds of other circumstances where people are trying to sell you something: The college professor who misleads his students because the real facts don't support his political agenda, the auto mechanic who tells you the wheel is going to fall of your car if you don't pay him $500 to flush the radiator, the electronic store representative who tries to sell your grandmother a high end stereo VCR when you have told him that she only has a 13 inch television that doesn't put out stereo sound and on and on...

So What's the point, you ask? What can I do about it?

* **Don't buy in!** Don't listen. Reduce your exposure to a runaway stream of information. Don't just rock along in auto pilot. Think about what you're doing.

* **Any information going through your mind that isn't relevant to your life** merely causes mental clutter which causes stress. If you're stressed, chances are you have this problem.

* **Turn off the news!** You don't need to know every detail of what is going on in the world. I have found that not following the news has greatly reduced the stress in my life. Yes, it is sad when a child drowns half a continent away, but unless I know the child or his family or unless it is reasonable to think the same will happen to my child, why do I need to know? It is just a cause for needless stress. It is important to be informed before you vote, but you can easily do some intentional research about the candidates shortly before an election rather than follow the daily barrage of news coverage.

"What if something happens that I really need to know about?" You will always know people who will tell you things you absolutely need to know. On September 11th, my brother in law called to tell me to watch the news. Keep in contact with your neighbors. If something happens in your neighborhood, they will tell you. Then, if you want to know the details, go to the most reliable source of news you can find and seek out only that story.

* **Don't watch so much television.** This is important especially if you watch a lot of high stress television. Police crime dramas, abrasive TV talk shows and "He Said, She Said" reality shows will raise your stress levels. Too much of any kind of television time bleeds away hours of your life that you may later wish you still had.

* **When you feel the urge to buy something, stop** and ask yourself if you're being brainwashed or if you really need that thing you want to buy. Chances are if you have to have it RIGHT NOW, it's an impulse buy. Put it

off for a while. Weigh the value. I have found that if I delay a purchase, I almost always realize that I don't need or really want it.

* **When someone tells you something that seems important,** don't just believe it, especially if the information causes you anxiety or has some impact on your belief system in general. If it is important, verify the information with a reliable source. I wish I had done this more in college, when I for a time believed unquestioningly the lies that some professors told me, even while they encouraged me to challenge beliefs for which I actually had solid evidence.

* **Don't "surf" the Internet because you're bored.** When you go to the Internet, make sure you have a purpose: You want information on a particular topic or you want to play a game or buy a song that gives you encouragement. If you just surf, though, you are just finding information to clutter your brain which will compound your stress.

* **When too much information causes stress,** it is expensive. Stressed people usually smoke, eat too much, develop various addictions or simply seek medical attention that they may not have otherwise needed. All these things cost money that stress free people don't feel compelled to spend.

* **When too much information causes stress,** it adversely affects your health. Spending the majority of your time under a high degree of stress leads to all kinds of medical problems that make life unpleasant and will probably lead to an early death.

Common sense is not so common. - Voltaire

Home Theater Heist

By Michael Kellam

To the reader: I wrote this story in 2000 to illustrate the value of weighing the cost of items before buying them. I know that some of the prices may not reflect today's prices, but if you read the entire story, the thought process still applies.

Have you ever thought that some particular purchase would save you money? I often hear people talk about how they can save money by purchasing something that will save them in other ways. A good example of this is a custom home theater system. Many of my movie buff friends, awed by snazzy displays in electronics stores have convinced themselves that there is no cost in this type of purchase. After all, it is difficult to find a first run movie theater that sells tickets for less than $6.50 each and many are substantially more. Surely, they reason, at say $8.00 per ticket, they would save money purchasing this system that attempts to approximate the theater experience. Is this really the case?

One particular friend purchased his system in stages. First he purchased the large screen television for a cost of around $2000. Then he purchased a mid range stereo system including a DVD player for another $2000. For these prices, surely the stereo would include speakers, but says my friend, that is not the case. He spent another $1500 purchasing speakers and a sub woofer because he likes the bass. My friend was telling me how he got a great deal because he purchased several of the components at once. He asserted that he "saved" several hundred dollars on the equipment and that the entire system would pay for itself since he would no longer incur the cost of seeing theatrical releases.

Considering his assertions, my curiosity got the best of my and I began crunching numbers. I added his equipment costs and figured that his system cost $5500.00. At $8.00 per movie, that means he would have to watch 688 films on his home theater before it would pay for itself. Not bad, you might think. He might see that many films in two years if he watched one every day. Of course, this assumes he is watching films that he would have seen in the theater but chose to view them on his home theater instead or else he wouldn't be saving money. My friend found that even with his home theater, he did not want to give up theatrical movies all together, so maybe it would take a little bit longer for the system to pay for itself.

What my friend never figured into his numbers was that he was going to have to have DVD's to watch on this new system. At the purchase price for DVD's, suddenly it would be cheaper for him to watch a movie in the theater. His system could never pay for itself. My friend decided that he would instead rent the DVD's from the local video store, where DVD's rent for about $4.00 each. If all of the DVD's he watches are rented, he only saves $4.00 over the price of watching the film in a theater. This means that we have to do the math all over again. Now for the system to pay for itself (dividing the $5500.00 system by the $4.00 savings), my friend would have to watch 1375 movies for the system to pay for itself. He would have to watch at least one movie every day for close to four years before the system pays for itself. Now my friend is serious about movies, but lets face it, one movie every day is a lot of movies.

My friend never considered that after a couple of years, the technology would be so much better that he would want a new one. Sure his system was great, but look what they have now. Still, the system has not paid for itself so he must press on. He never considered that if he had simply paid the eight bucks to see a theater movie every day that he would be $3000 ahead at this point and not in hock for this stupid home theater. Heck he could have gone to the theater AND bought popcorn every day!

What makes it worse is that my friend bought his system at one of those electronics stores with the 1 year same as cash. How can you beat that – no interest! What he didn't know was that if the balance isn't paid off by the end of the year, that the company charges all of the interest back to the date of the purchase as if it was never "same as cash". To add insult to injury, the credit company charges 29% interest on purchases. That means that in addition to the $5500.00 my friend paid, he also has to pay $1595 PER YEAR interest until it is paid off. If he only pays the minimum payment of $150 per month, it will take him 91 months (7 1⁄2 years) to pay off the system. The total cost of the system is then $13647 including $8147 in interest. This means that including the $4.00 savings per movie, he will have to watch 3412 movies before the system pays for itself. That is a heck of a lot of movies. If my friend watched a movie every day, it would take him more than nine years for the system to pay for itself. In this case, my friend could have paid full price to watch movies every day at the theater for more than nine years. In fact, the system is not really paying for itself if my friend would not otherwise have actually paid the $8.00 every day for nine years to see that many films. It also does not take into consideration that most people see at least SOME movies in discount theaters. If my friend would have seen a film in a discount theater, he would actually be spending more for each movie he chose to view on his home theater.

What I have not mentioned here is that my friend works a job that pays him $20,000 per year. If he pays cash for the system (NOT using a credit card), he will have had to work over three months for no other reason but to pay for his home theater. If he uses a credit card, he will have had to work for more than 8 months to pay for the system. Now, I don't know about you, but if I could take 3-8 months off of work and still live at the same standard of living, I would rather do that than go to a job and work more for someone else so I can "save" money purchasing a home theater that might not pay even for itself for nine years.

I am not saying that home theaters are bad. I am simply saying that you should consider carefully the cost of something before you purchase it. I personally would not purchase such a system when I can see a film in glorious Technicolor on the big screen as it was meant to be seen (in 2.35:1 wide screen of course). If you feel that it is worth it to you to spend the money on such a system, it is your prerogative to spend it on whatever you wish to spend (keeping in mind that you must want it more than that other thing you can't afford after you have bought it). So go enjoy the movie! And say "Hi" to the ticket taker for me!

> AT&T is now offering a new service that allows you to pay your bills through your TV screen by using your remote control. So instead of saying, "The check's in the mail," people are going to say, "Hey, I wanted to pay, but I couldn't find the remote.
>
> - Jay Leno

It's Your Choice

I was down on my hands and knees for the third time that day wiping up the trail of mud the kids and dog had left on my white kitchen floor. With each swipe of the rag my grumbling got worse until finally in a fit of self pity I threw down the rag and started whining "Dear God why does so and so have a nice concrete driveway and I don't?" In a gentle quiet voice He answered, "The choice is yours. Do you want to stay at home and clean up muddy footprints from your kids or work long hours in an office all day to earn money for a new concrete driveway?"

I learned a very important principle that day. Almost everything that happens in my life is because of the choices I make. Nothing was more important to me than staying at home with my children. Because of that choice, it meant we couldn't have a lot of extras that we wanted. I had no right to be envious of my friend who had a new home, car and a closet full of designer clothes. She worked long hard hours, but missed out on a lot of special things with her children in order to help pay for it all. In the same way she had no right to envy me because I had chosen to stay home with my children and to clean muddy floors all day. We both had made our choices and our own sacrifices.

We get many e-mails saying "I wish I could stay at home but we can't live on one paycheck alone". Yes you can. The choice is yours and, as I said, every choice has its sacrifices. It is just a matter of deciding what sacrifices you are willing to make. I lived in Idaho. I had a job I liked, a home I liked and it was less expensive for me to live there. But my family (especially my grand kids) lived in Kansas. I had a choice to make. I chose Kansas. I gave up a nice home, a great climate, and a better financial situation but I gained what I really wanted and needed -- to be with my family.

Our choices aren't always major life changing ones. My son-in-law drives "The White Car". The white car is slowly being overtaken by rust. There are no springs left in the drivers seat so you are basically sitting on the floor while you are driving. I wouldn't be a bit surprised if I looked up one day and saw him driving down the street with nothing more then a steering wheel, 4 tires, and an engine left.

My daughter asked him the other day, " If you had the choice to buy a brand new car (which costs the same as a years salary of his) or to take off work for a year which would you choose? He chose taking the time off. He said that even though it is not the newest car and that everything didn't work the way it would in a new car, it is still a car that gets him from one place to another. You see either way he had to make a sacrifice. It was just a matter of what he wanted to sacrifice. Eventually, it will not be practical to keep "The White Car", but I know that when that time comes, he will not buy a brand new car, but a low price used car that will not require him to go into debt.

So the next time you pull that credit card out to pay for something you want or need, think about what sacrifices you will be making for your choice. Are you sacrificing you and your spouse's peace of mind because of the stress and burden you place yourself under trying to pay for it? Are you sacrificing curling up with a good book, having dinner with your family or spending a romantic evening with your spouse? Is the cost worth it?

Why Ask Why?

Why do we press harder on a remote control when we know the batteries are getting weak?

Why do banks charge a fee on "insufficient funds" when they know there is not enough?

Why doesn't glue stick to the bottle?

If people evolved from apes, why are there still apes?

Is there ever a day that mattresses are not on sale?

If You Want to Work at Home, Be Creative!

You want to stay home with your children but due to circumstances beyond your control you are their sole support. What jobs can you do and still be at home for the kids? There are many magazines out there that have lists of stay at home jobs but they don't seem to work out for a lot of individuals. I don't think they work for two reasons:

First, many people haven't really made up their minds that their children's emotional and spiritual needs are greater than their children's material wants. Being present in your children's lives is more important than buying them things. When I made up my mind that the most important and best thing for my children was for me to be there for them, that became my main goal. Then when a job came along, I didn't consider the best job the one that paid the most, but the one that gave me the most time with my kids.

The second reason moms have trouble finding things that allow them to stay home is that each individual's circumstances, gifts or talents and needs vary so greatly. It is difficult for anyone to suggest a handful of solutions that will work for everyone. For example, at one point I was working at a very well paying receptionist job. When my daughter had a long term knee injury, I had to leave that job for a job that paid less because it left me free to pick her up at all different times of day. Another time when both my children were seriously ill and I couldn't leave them at all, I stayed home and ironed clothes for other people.

I became like any Olympic skater or swimmer, trying to achieve my goal. I got up early and worked long, hard days. I sacrificed much to obtain my goal. I overcame my natural shyness and told everyone I met that I ironed, baked cookies, built piano parts or whatever they needed. I did that in order to find the work that I needed to obtain my goal, which was to be there for my kids.

If you are stumped at what kinds of jobs or things you can do to stay at home and earn money here are a few suggestions:

Think about things that are a little out of the ordinary. Don't do crafts!! You usually spend more time, money and energy than you will ever earn. That's why they call them "starving" artists.

Try to think of needs that people need fulfilled. I did ironing and found out that I made more money doing that than I did as a receptionist. At one point I had a women who brought me her groceries, disposable pans and her favorite recipes. I cooked 15-20 of her favorite meals and she would store them in her freezer for the month. If you have excessive garden produce, sell it to the restaurants in your area. You can grow herbs very easily and restaurants love fresh herbs.

Don't limit yourself to working "at home" if you can do something that fits your need to be "at home". Don't be afraid to ask for what you want. If you would love to work in the school cafeteria because the work has the same hours that your children are in school, don't be afraid to ask if there is an opening. If you can sew, inquire at decorating shops. A lot of times they need seamstresses who can do basic sewing to work flexible part time hours. A lot of businesses need someone to run errands and you can often adapt their hours to your needs.

If you're thinking, "but I have a degree," consider that if your degree is not providing you with a job that allows you to be at home with your kids, you should throw it out the window and stop using it as an excuse for not finding the right job. Remember your education, high standard of living and material things are not what are important here -- raising your children is the important thing.

If you want the rainbow, you gotta put up with the rain. - Dolly Parton

Things To Look Out For If You Want To Work At Home

Julie writes: Hi, I just came across your site and find it very helpful and interesting. **I wondered if you had any ideas or information on work at home opportunities.** I am overwhelmed and confused at all that is out there . How do I determine what is legit and what is a scam? Specifically the Paid to do surveys online and also Mystery Shopping ads. I would appreciate any info. Thank You.

Hi Julie, **We aren't familiar with all of the possible work at home opportunities, but here are a few things to keep in mind:**

Be clear about what the company wants you to do and what your benefit will be. Ask a lot of questions. If they won't tell you what kind of work you will be doing, I would keep looking.

If you find a company you want to work for, check them out. Do Google search for the company name and see what's out there about the company. Beware: If there are a number of web sites describing bad business practices, it is probably a bad sign. Find out where the company is located and check the better business bureau. If it is a corporation, contact the secretary of state's office in the state where the company offices are and see if they are listed in "good standing".

Don't do anything where the company asks for money up front. For work at home jobs, there really isn't a good reason for a company to ask you to pay them. Sometimes the "job" is really a product that they are selling you. They may advertise "work at home" and instead of a job, what they're really offering is a directory of companies you can call to try to get jobs with no guarantee that you will get one with your "investment".

Don't give personal information without thoroughly checking out the company. There are many people out there looking for ways to get credit card, bank account and social security numbers. Never give out this kind of sensitive information unless you have thoroughly checked out the company, are certain who is receiving the information and are comfortable that the information is secure.

Be cautious of "too good to be true" income projections. If the income seems tremendous for a small amount of work, something is wrong. If all you have to do is sit at home and wait for checks to hit your mailbox, they're not being straight with you.

Multi Level Marketing (also called "Network Marketing") - Be very careful if you consider this type of work. Generally, when a person tries to recruit you for this type of work, the person will do everything possible not to tell you what type of work it is until you meet with him in person. That alone should make you suspicious.

It is possible to make money with this type of work, but it requires a tremendous amount of work to get a large income. I knew someone who did make a lot of money doing this. He said that in order to make a lot of money, he and his wife both ended up working 80 hours per week. He said that they didn't really have a life anymore and that it put so much pressure on their marriage that they nearly divorced over it. I think this illustrates that no matter what you do, you can't get something for nothing.

I can also tell you that when I was younger, I worked as a temp contracted for two days to a Multi Level Marketing company stuffing bonus checks into envelopes. During the two full days of work, virtually every bonus check I saw was for less than $5.00 and then once in a while, I saw one for $10,000. That is because only the one person was willing to do the work necessary for the big money. Everyone else was led to believe that the "opportunity" was the equivalent of a lottery ticket - big return with no work. Unfortunately, it doesn't work that way.

Paid Online Surveys - We recommend that you pass on these. I talked to a college student recently who said she made money answering surveys online, but I don't think this is an effective way to make a reliable income. She sounded like she just needed a little extra cash for the weekends. In exchange for filling out surveys, you generally have to request sales calls from companies and agree for companies to call, e-mail and mail you all sorts of solicitations. Usually, the time involved and the hassle of dealing with the solicitations is not worth the money.

Mystery Shoppers - Often, companies work with consulting groups who send mystery shoppers into their stores to evaluate products and services. I have known people who did this and they seemed happy with it. The pay was not great, but was roughly equivalent to a lot of part time jobs and did allow for flexibility. If you do a little research on the company and it seems legitimate, this can be a good opportunity.

Home Manufacturing - Some companies have work at home programs where they send you raw materials and you create a product. It might be a company that makes dolls and sends you the materials to make them. When the job is done, you send the product back and get paid. Most of what I have seen in this realm is very low paying work.

The best home businesses are home grown businesses. If you want to make money, try to find something that you are certain people need, but can't easily get and then find a way to give it to them. Jill has done ironing and sewing for people and sold homemade cookies. Tawra has grown and sold herbs, potpourri, crafts and cookbooks. We don't recommend art and craft items because too many people are willing to "sell" them at no profit because their motivation is primarily hobby centered.

Another thing that many people have success with is Ebay Selling. If you decide to do this, don't pay to buy somebody's "system". There are books that give tips to do this that you can buy or check out at the library. Try to think of items that you can get for a better price than the price the same items are selling for on Ebay. I wouldn't do it if you only made a dollar or two on an auction. We've known lots of people that had success with this and we have had some success doing this in the past, too.

If you're passionate about a particular subject and you have a website or blog, you can get extra money by putting ads on your site or by selling books you particularly like as an affiliate.

Many publishers offer affiliate programs that pay affiliates around 50% for e-book sales or around 30% for sales of "traditional" books. The way it works is any time the publisher sells something that you referred as an affiliate, you get paid. If you know somebody who has a book that you like, ask if they have an affiliate program. You can also check ClickBank, where there are many publishers offering affiliate programs but you would want to investigate the opportunity carefully to make sure you want to be recommending the item you choose.

If you decide to try advertising, Google Adsense is an easy and free system you can integrate in your site. In order to make money with

Adsense, you have to have a certain amount of traffic on your site, so if Aunt Ruth is the only one reading your Blog, ads are not for you ;-). If you do try adsense, be sure to monitor the ads periodically. You can block ads from specific advertisers, which we try to do for anyone who seems to be offering "too good to be true" deals.

10 Signs that you've had too much of the New Millennium:

1. You try to enter your password on the microwave.

2. You haven't played solitaire with a real deck of cards in years.

3. You have a list of 15 phone numbers to reach your family of 3.

4. You e-mail your son in his room to tell him that dinner is ready, and he emails you back "What's for dinner?"

5. You chat several times a day with a stranger from South Africa, but you haven't spoken to your next door neighbor yet this year.

6. You buy a computer and a week later it is out of date and now sells for half the price you paid.

7. Cleaning up the dining area means getting the fast food bags out of the back seat of your car.

8. Your idea of being organized is multiple colored post-it notes.

9. You really get excited about a 1.7% pay increase.

10. Free food left over from meetings is your staple diet.

Grocery Savings

Stop Cutting Coupons and Start Saving!

Many of us feel overwhelmed by debt and don't know how to start climbing out of it. For others it's a misconception that the more money you earn the easier it is to save. My husband and I paid off $20,000 of credit card debt and medical bills in 5 years on an average income of $22,000 a year.

Here is how you can save over $10,000 in just one year cutting a few things from your grocery bill. If you're trying to save so you can stay home with your kids, put a down payment on a house, pay off some credit card debt or just have some emergency money, here are 10 ways to do it without depriving yourself. The total annual savings will amaze you!
When it comes to saving money in your household budget, the little things really do add up. Look how much you would save in a year if you cut out just **ONE** thing.

ITEM	PRICE	HOW OFTEN	COST PER YEAR
1 bag chips	$2.99/bag	1 week	$155.00
1-6 pack soda	$2.00	1/week	$104.00
Bottled Water	$1.25	1/day	$456.25
1 liter soda	$1.00	1/day	$365.00
purchased at convenience store			
Reduce meat	$3.00/lb. (1.5 lbs.)	2 nights/week	$468.00
1 gourmet coffee	$3.65	1/day	$1332.25
Eating out for a family of 4:			
Dinner	$30.00	1/week	$1560.00
Dinner	$40.00	1/week	$2080.00
Lunch	$5.00/person	20 days/month	$1200.00
Pizza delivered	$20.00	1/ week	$1040.00
1 cup juice per	$1.50	1/week	$547.50
person family of 4			
Fruit leather	$2.50	1/week	$130.00
1 box granola	$4.00	1/week	$208.00
1 snack cake	$1.25	1/day	$456.25

Total if you cut all these out: **$10,102.73**

Save on Groceries Before You Leave Home

One of the easiest ways to save money on your grocery bill starts before you even leave the house. It's no extra work, you don't have to deprive yourself of anything and you don't have to clip any coupons. What is it? Stop wasting food.

Better planning keeps you from throwing away so much food, saving you money!

On average most families throw away 50% of the food they buy. If you have trouble believing that then watch your family's eating habits for the next few days. How many times did your child eat only half of his lunch or dinner or drink only half of his glass of milk or juice? How much food gets thrown away when you wash dishes? How many fruits and vegetables have rotted and been tossed? How much meat have you thrown away because it is freezer burned? And what about those leftovers in the fridge or the cartons of sour milk?

If this is you, do you realize if you spend $400 a month on groceries you are literally throwing $200 of it into the trash? What would you think if someone you knew took two $100 bills and threw them away?!? That would make dumpster divers out of the most genteel among us.

Here are some ideas on how to help you to stop the waste:

1. Only fill a child's (or adult's) glass half full if they normally don't drink it all. You can always give them more when that is gone. If they do have left over milk or juice at the end of the meal put it in the fridge for them to finish at another time.

2. When you get ready to cook a piece of meat like a roast or chicken, plan ahead. For example, when I take a roast out to thaw I don't think, "Ok, we'll have roast and mashed potatoes tonight." But I think "I will have roast and mashed potatoes tonight, Bar-B-Q beef tomorrow and beef and noodles the next night." That way you won't find yourself three days later gazing guiltily at that dying leftover roast thinking, "I really should do something with this but what?" and then end up throwing it out a week later.

3. Check your fridge the night before you go to the grocery store. That way you can plan your menus and choose what to buy based on the leftovers you have.

4. If all else fails, make one night a week as leftover night. That's when you set out all your odds and ends of leftovers for everyone to polish off. This is especially good if you do it the night before you buy groceries because this leaves your fridge empty for the new things you are buying tomorrow.

Joke of the Day

A mother was preparing pancakes for her sons, Kevin 5, and Ryan 3.

The boys began to argue over who would get the first pancake. Their mother saw the opportunity for a moral lesson.

"If Jesus were sitting here, He would say, 'Let my brother have the first pancake, I can wait.'

Kevin turned to his younger brother and said, "Ryan, you be Jesus!"

Are Warehouse Stores Wearing Out Your Wallet?

It's Saturday morning. With grocery list in hand, you drag a very unwilling family out to the car where you proceed to take them on a mega shopping spree at Sam's or Costco.

Marching down each isle you tell your family members "We need 3 cases of corn, 4 cases of green beans and -- Oh! That's a good deal on peanut butter so let's get 3 gallons. Of course Susie, your can get a bag of cookies. They are so cheap! ...and Billy you can have a few bags of your favorite chips! Yum! Oh look -- samples! These taste great. Let's get some! What a great buy on chicken – we need 20..."

At the dog food aisle the excitement mounts as each member of the family grabs a corner of the 50 lb. bag of dog food to stack on top of the basket. (We won't mention you only have 1 toy poodle at home.) After waiting in line and waiting in line and waiting in line you push your agonizingly heavy and overloaded baskets out to the car. Getting everything into the trunk of the car makes putting together a 1,000 piece puzzle a breeze, but finally home you go.

After you lug everything into the house, it's time to spend the next few hours repackaging things for the freezer. You double wrap your 20 chickens (they could be in that freezer for quite awhile) and frantically try to find places for everything else in your cupboards and panty. By the time you are done, you are so exhausted that you couldn't begin to lift a finger to cook, so you all go out to eat.

A few weeks later you gingerly sniff the gallon of half used peanut butter as you try to decide if that strange taste is because it has gone rancid or simply because you are sick of peanut butter. You threw out that partially used gallon of maple syrup yesterday because it had sugared and was looking really strange. You still have ten of your chickens left but if you bathe them in some spicy sauce you are pretty sure your family won't notice the freezer burned taste. In spite of having to throw out most of the 50 lbs. of dog food (after a growing family of mice had invaded it), you're sure you saved money because "they" said you would.

Time and time again, people ask "can you really save money at Sam's or Costco?" I usually answer "not any more so then any place else". I have checked prices several different times and factoring everything in, I have found no exceptional savings.

Here are some tips to help you decide if a warehouse store is for you:

1. Do your homework and compare prices. Buying in bulk is not always cheaper. You really save by checking and comparing prices. I was at Costco one day where there was a display of two Clorox one gallon bottles for $1.98 AFTER rebate. I stood there amazed as people grabbed up this "great deal." I knew I could get that same Clorox for $.98 a gallon at my regular discount store and I didn't have to mess with a rebate, pay postage or lug 2 gallons of Clorox shrink wrapped together to my car.

2. Don't buy impulsively just because it sounds like a good deal. Say you can get 12 bottles of sunscreen for a great price. Think it through before you buy. If your family only uses one bottle sunscreen a year, that means you will be storing sunscreen for 12 years, not to mention that most of the sunscreen will expire long before then.

3. In most homes up to one half of food people buy gets thrown out. Even though my story was somewhat tongue-in-cheek, there is a certain amount of truth to it. If your family of four eats pancakes once a week, that gallon of syrup is going to last you a VERY long time. You might also consider that unless dry goods and freezer items are very carefully stored, they will go bad or get bugs in them. Remember to buy the size appropriate for your family.

4. You need to be very well organized to buy in bulk. All the shows and magazine articles about organizing suggest that most of us are organizationally challenged. Finding places to store everything and then carefully keeping track of what you have is critical if you want to use it all before it spoils.

5. Most people usually spend more then they originally planned on things they don't need. This never saves money. We taste samples and so often end up buying. If this is you, be careful. Maybe sampling is a bad idea (unless you're making lunch of it)!

If you have ten kids, run a day care or are buying for an organization then you almost have to buy in bulk. If you have a small or average sized family, you will probably save as much shopping for sales at your regular grocery store or discount store. The key is to do the math and evaluate your practical needs. You have to decide for yourself if buying at warehouse stores actually saves you money or just creates more work.

Calories That Don't Count

Dieting is a lot easier when you factor in recently determined calorie counting principles. The following are calories that don't count:

CUSTOM MADE FOOD: Anything somebody made "just for you" must be eaten regardless of the calories because to do otherwise would be rude. But don't worry, because the calories don't count.

FOOD EATEN QUICKLY: If you are rushed through a meal, the entire meal doesn't count. Conversely, if you have ordered something fattening and now regret it, you can minimize its calories by gulping it down.

OTHER PEOPLE'S FOOD: A chocolate mousse that you did not order has no calories. Therefore, have your companion order dessert and you taste half of it.

Save Money Shopping at Aldi

Aldi is a great store where you can save lots of money!

I spend $250 a month on groceries. One of the best things I do to keep my budget is to do most of my food shopping at Aldi. You can get a good price, get in and get out fast and you don't have to mess with using coupons.

Aldi is a small discount warehouse store. It is not an outlet store and does not sell outdated or rejected products. They offer a double your money back guarantee for all of their products. If you don't like it, they will give you your money back plus a new item. The foods are mostly Aldi brand foods. The Aldi brand is usually very good quality. I have only had one or two items where my family preferred the name brand over the Aldi brand.

The savings are significant. On a lot of items, I can save $1 or more over the price at a regular grocery store. Here's an example: Chocolate chips at the local supermarket cost $1.99. Aldus regular price is .99. White bread in the supermarket costs $1. Aldus bread costs .59. Whole grain bread costs $2.59 in regular grocery store, but Aldi's regular price is $1.29.

Aldi stores are all over the world. Here is the link to the Aldi website to see if one is near you: http://www.aldi.com

There are a few rules to follow that keep their prices low:

1. They accept only cash, debit or food stamps.

2. They don't accept coupons.

3. You have to pay a .25 deposit to get a shopping basket. There is a little quarter machine on the basket. When you return your basket, it gives you the quarter back. This keeps prices down because they don't have to pay someone to get baskets.

4. You bag your own groceries. Bring your own bags. Put all your extra plastic sacks in an empty tissue box and bring it with you. You can also

use the boxes they have there for free. If they don't have any boxes available and you forget your bags, they charge $.10 per bag for you to buy them.

When the checker checks you out, she puts the groceries right back into the basket and you have to take them to a separate counter to bag or box them. I usually roll the basket out to the car and box it there so that I can strap my 2 year old into his car seat while I pack the groceries. That way I don't have to chase him around while I'm trying to get packed and I get packed up in five minutes instead of 10 or 15.

5. To get the freshest produce, ask when their truck comes and go shopping the next morning.

6. Be prepared. The checkers check you out very fast. I have timed it and on average it's 2-3 minutes check out time with a full basket of groceries. It may be a little awkward the first time getting used to a different way of shopping, but once you do it once or twice, the savings are addicting!

By shopping at Aldi, I get two weeks worth of groceries (excluding meat -- I buy it elsewhere) for $100.00. I am in and out of the store in 30 minutes including bagging my groceries. Plan a little longer the first time as you learn your way around the store. Try it a couple of times and see if you grocery bill doesn't go down!

From our Inbox:
Dear Tawra,
I just wanted to thank you for your article on shopping at Aldi's. I recently shopped there for the first time and I was very pleased with the wide selection they had available and the prices are FANTASTIC. Shopping there has already reduced the amount of money I spend for groceries to feed my family of 4 (which includes two VERY hungry teenaged boys), and I look forward to saving more as I continue to shop there each week for my groceries. Thank you for you wonderful web site and I look forward to readying more tips and articles to save money.

Sincerely, Shellia Jean A.

Have a Cool Glass of Cash!

If I said I would give you $150 extra a month to help you pay off your credit cards, lose weight and help your family become healthier, would you accept it? Does it sound too good to be true? The average American family spends 1/4-1/3 of their monthly grocery bill on things to drink but can't find any extra money to pay off their credit cards.

Do you buy sodas, coffee, tea, juice and milk, plus all the things that go into these drinks like creamer, flavorings and sugar? Do you grab a glass of soda, juice or milk instead of a cold glass of water? You may even argue that juice and milk are good for your children but fertilizer (food for you grass) is good for your lawn. We all know that too much fertilizer will kill it and if you don't water it, it will die. I'm beginning to wonder if most of us are more concerned about making sure our yards are watered then our children. Of course they need some milk but like everything else do it in moderation.

Here are few tips to cut the costs of the drinks in your home and find some extra money to pay off your credit cards:

Find out how much milk is actually needed for your child. The USDA recommends that children under 5 get three to four servings of dairy per day. That is 2 cups of milk OR one serving equals one slice of cheese OR 1/2 container of yogurt. Don't forget milk added to cereal.

Juice is just sugar water. Eat the whole fruit instead and give one glass of juice as a treat for breakfast or snack.

Limit the number of glasses of milk or juice given a day. After the allotted amount they get nothing else but water. If they are used to drinking it for meals, either give them one glass (1/2 cup) and when it's gone they drink water or have them drink water first and then milk after they finish their meal.

Use small juice glasses. They give the appearance of more.

Don't fill their sippy cups with juice or milk. Give them water instead.

If you put some milk in a cup and they don't drink it all, put it in the fridge until later.

Limit sodas to a treat once or twice a week.

Don't dilute your juice with extra water. Not only does this not taste very well but by "stretching" the juice you teach your kids bad eating habits by giving into their demands for juice instead of giving them water.

Keep water in the fridge. After water has set, the chlorine evaporates and the water tastes better cold.

Add a small amount of lemon juice to your water if you don't like the taste.

Be careful to shop wisely. Sometimes buying name brand flavored or specialty coffees on sale costs less than making your own.

Use powdered milk instead of creamer in coffee or tea or try mixing your creamer half and half with dry milk.

After making coffee save the coffee filter and the coffee grounds in the maker. Add your coffee for the next day on top of the old grounds. This way you can use each filter 2 or 3 times. Buy a reusable coffee filter. They last for years.

If you run out of coffee filters use a paper towel until you can get to the store to buy more.

You don't always have to make a full pot of coffee. Just make one or 2 cups at time.

Save extra coffee in a thermos instead of making a new batch or buy a smaller coffee maker.

To make flavored tea add a package of flavored drink mix to each pot of tea.

For leftover soda, combine 2 cups of flat soda with 1 package of unflavored or same flavored gelatin to make a rich flavored gelatin. This is particularly good with root beer, orange and grape sodas.

What is an Appropriate Food Budget?

Elise from Kelowna, British Columbia writes:

Hi Tawra and Jill,
My husband and I are saving hard for a mortgage down-payment and we are trying to stick to a budget, but I don't know what is an appropriate amount of money to allot for food per month. I try to get everything on sale and in bulk, as well as utilizing free sources of fruit and vegetables. (Here in the Okanagan they are all over!) Could you give me some advice about this? It is just the two of us -- we have no children yet.

Thank you for the help, and also thank you for this inspiring website. I always read your articles and they boost my resolve to be as frugal as I can while still living life richly.

Thanks again, Elise

Tawra:
The answer to your question depends on a lot of factors. I can't really give you a dollar amount because the price of food varies from state to state and from the US to Canada. When Mike and I were living alone we spent $125 a month on groceries (US dollars). My best advice is each day or week think about where you can cut a little more from your bill. No matter how much you cut, there is only so far you can go. Eventually you will get to an average point and this will be a steady bill for you. Then focus on how you can save in other areas.

Generally, if you cut out the convenience foods and go to restaurants as little as possible you will be well on the way. Since you are saving extra hard right now, I would cut out all of the restaurant trips except maybe on your anniversary and try for no expensive convenience foods. Then, when you have saved what you want to save, ease up on those things a little if you like.

Also, keep in mind that it may be worth it at times to use convenience foods if you have an opportunity to make more money with the time you save. For example, if you and your husband can work some overtime this week and it pays well, but it eliminates the time you have to prepare meals for the week, it might be worth buying some TV dinners. Still, whenever possible, I'd prepare some freezer meals ahead of time when things are slow to make up for the time you may not have later.

It sounds like you are well on your way to getting it as low as you can. I hope you get your down payment quickly!

More Calories That Don't Count

INGREDIENTS IN COOKING: Chocolate chips are fattening. So are chocolate chip cookies! However, chocolate chips eaten while making chocolate chip cookies have no calories whatsoever. Therefore, make chocolate chip cookies often but don't eat them.

LEFTOVERS: An extra hamburger, a hotdog butt, half a Twinkie, anything intended for the garbage has no calories regardless of what happens to it in the kitchen.

TV FOOD: Anything eaten in front of a TV has no calories. This may have something to do with the radiation leakage, which negates not only the calories in the food but also all recollection of having eaten it. In fact, entire " no-calories dinners" are now manufactured and frozen for this purpose.

ANYTHING SMALLER THAN ONE INCH: contains no calories to speak of. For example, chocolate kisses, cubes of cheese, or maraschino cherries.

CHILDREN'S FOOD: Anything purchased, produced or intended for minors is calorie-free when eaten by adults. This category covers a wide range, beginning with a spoonful of baby tapioca-consumed for demonstration purposes-up to and including cookies baked and sent to college.

Shopping On A Budget
When You're Tired

Robbi writes: **I have fibromyalgia and a host of other ailments, most of them chronic.** There are days when I just want to grab the first things I see and get out of the store and back home to rest. How do you get your shopping done for the week without killing yourself and destroying your budget in the process?

Jill: **I know it can be very hard to go to the grocery store when you are sick.** My daughter and I once went, parked in the store parking lot and had to turn around and drive right back home because we were too exhausted after just making the short drive to get there. Boy, did we feel dumb. Here are a couple of ideas that may help a little.

First, always keep a list. That may be hard because for me, by the time I find a pencil, I usually forget what I was going to write down. HA!HA! The list helps you not only to remember things, but also helps you decide what to buy. I am usually so sick at the store that nothing sounds good, so making myself buy just what is on my list helps.

I also go to the smallest grocery store in my area. Walking up and down long aisles just kills me. I like Aldi's because it not only helps me save money but is smaller.

You may find it easier to buy a month's worth of staples all at once. Then, just go once a week to buy the fresh items. The fresh items are on the outside wall of most grocery stores so I can sometimes walk that distance if I don't have to go up and down each isle where the staples are.

Make a floor plan of your store. Some stores have floor plans already made for your use. When you buy items that always seem hard to find (for me it is syrup), make a note of the location on your floor plan. Then you don't have to wear yourself out wandering the aisles aimlessly.

Price Match - Some superstores will match the prices of their competitors ads. I take my ads in and purchase all my sale items at one store. Then I don't have to go from store to store purchasing the exceptional deals. I can get the sale price all at one store. Ask if your store will do this and it can save time and money.

To help save money, ask your butcher when he marks down the meat. The same goes for produce and bakery items. That way you can plan to do your shopping when the bargains are right there. You don't have to go hunting for them.

Keep you meals simple. Don't feel guilty if you get to the grocery store and only have the energy to buy milk and cereal. Guilt drains you. Once I stopped fighting and feeling guilty about what I couldn't do and what other people would think about what I wasn't doing, I actually started having some good days.

Why do people constantly return to the refrigerator with hopes that something new to eat will have materialized?

Make Life Easier Without Eating Out

I have been saying this for years and I just heard it on Oprah so I'm sure that makes it true! Going out to eat is one of the biggest mistakes people make with their money. Most people would experience a radical change in their finances if they would cut back on eating out even a couple of times a week, let alone all together.

I think that the main reason that people go out to eat is for the convenience. I hope to show you how eating at home can be convenient, too.

We seem to be people of extremes and that definitely spills over into our thoughts about meals. We have the idea that there are only two choices when it comes to providing dinner for our families. The first is to go out to eat and not lift a finger. The second is to become Betty Crocker, an Amish grandmother and Martha Stewart all rolled into one. Oh! And don't forget to roll in Mr. Clean for the clean up!

It doesn't have to be an all or nothing situation. For those of you who are extremely frugal, some of these suggestions might seem wasteful, but if making everything homemade is overwhelming to the point that you won't be able to keep it up, try some of these suggestions to make dinner easier without eating out.

1. Make meals easier by using convenience items. Even if you use nothing but convenience items for your entire meal, it is still less expensive than going out to eat. You don't need to make homemade bread, muffins, biscuits, or cookies. Buy them already made. You can even buy things like French bread, already sliced and buttered and ready to heat. It's perfectly OK to use bagged lettuce, baby carrots, or anything frozen.

2. Keep it simple. Our grandmothers didn't spend as many hours slaving away in the kitchen as we think they did. Instead of homemade bread or yeast rolls, the everyday meal included store-bought white or wheat bread on a plate with butter and jam. Grandma would open a jar of applesauce, a can of green beans or a jar of assorted pickles. She would toss a simple salad and have all her side dishes for that meal prepared quickly.

For years our family raved about my grandmother-in-law's great homemade noodles. One day when I asked her for her recipe, she pulled me to one side, laughing, and said "No one else knows this, but I always use frozen noodles!" Our grandmothers knew the secret. It didn't have to be complicated, gourmet, or elaborate for our families to enjoy a meal. It just had to be good, there had to be lots of it and it had to be made with love.

It takes only a couple of minutes to slice an orange, apple or banana and lay them on a platter. Throw in some unpeeled small red potatoes to boil, slice pre-cooked ham, heat up a box of fish fillets or lay out a variety of deli meats and cheeses for everyone to make their own hoagies. It can be as simple as that.

3. Make clean up easy. I line almost every pan I use with aluminum foil or parchment paper, whether I'm roasting a chicken or baking biscuits, cookies or tater tots. I line every casserole dish too.

Use paper plates and bowls if it helps. Use disposable pans when you can. You can usually find lots of them on sale around the holidays. Many people feel a lot of guilt connected with using anything disposable. If you are one of them, I give you permission here and now to use these things. Besides, when you eat out, just as much stuff gets thrown away. It's just that other people throw it away for you. I would much rather see you at home using paper plates and disposable pans with your family than having to work many hours of over time to pay for dinner out.

Relax, enjoy your meal. Your family and pocketbook will thank you.

Meals in 30 Minutes or Less

I was having dinner at my son's house the other night and my daughter-in-law had fixed "old fashioned" baked potatoes. You know in the oven and not the microwave. Boy, they were good. It seems so many things taste better slow cooked in the oven.

We started talking about how much longer it took to cook them in the oven compared to the microwave. That started me thinking. Yes, it does take longer in actual cooking time but in some ways it is easier. When I bake potatoes in the oven, I get them ready and in the oven an hour before dinner and forget about them until dinner is ready. Then, all I have to do is set them on the table and dinner is served.

When I microwave them, I tend to start cleaning them and preparing them at the same time that I'm trying to make a salad and heat up the veggies. While I'm doing all of that, I have to remember to keep turning the potatoes and if I am cooking several, I have to put a few in the microwave and when they are done, pull them out and add more, all of this at the same time that I am trying to prepare the rest of the meal.

Why is it that, even though we have faster methods of cooking our meals, they seem to have become more frenzied and hurried than years ago? Then it dawned on me -- With the introduction of the microwave and the idea that meals can be prepares in 30 minutes, most people do nothing to prepare or plan their meals until 30 minutes before they are going to eat. So 30 minutes before dinner you find yourself trying to thaw something, cook it, and slap it on the table and at the same time talk and deal with tired, hungry, cranky kids. Let's not forget how exhausted you are at this time of day, too.

We need to warm up our ovens and start using them again the way our grandmothers use to do. Here are some tips and ideas that prove that cooking meals in a conventional oven instead of a microwave can be just as quick and easy, not to mention how much more delicious they taste and smell.

I think we underestimate the power of coming home and smelling something yummy cooking. We automatically seem to relax, feeling that "all is well with the world". I really think it can change the whole atmosphere of your home for the evening.

I am not living in a dream world. You can fix meals the way our grandmothers did. I hear some readers saying, "Our grandmothers weren't ever as busy as we are and so they had time to fix large meals." I can hear our grandmothers chuckling at that statement. My husband's grandmother had to help on the farm from early in the morning until evening. She took care of a large home garden, canned, cleaned house every day, did laundry without a washer or dryer and still provided meals not only for her family, but up to 20 farm hands as well. She had to do it all without a refrigerator, microwave, or a grocery store and the nearest water was a mile away from her house.

My mother-in-law would go to work as early as 7 am and work until 9 pm 6 days a week, but she still managed to make three large meals each day. If you're thinking, "That's great if you want to spend all your spare time in the kitchen," consider that they spent less time in the kitchen than we do with less of the conveniences and still managed to have well balanced delicious meals each day.

What was their secret? They had never heard of 30 minute meals. Even if they had they would probably have laughed and wondered who would spend so much time on a meal? They knew that the key to a quick meal wasn't how fast you could cook, but how organized you were. You can easily have a meal on the table in 15 minutes if you are organized and plan ahead.

That doesn't mean microwave and frying everything to have a quick meal either. Slow cooking something in the oven not only makes things taste better but sometimes is quicker.

Our grandmothers' secret to quick meals:

* Keep your meals simple.

* Be organized.

* Decide what you are preparing the night or the morning before.

* Thaw anything you need the night or the morning before.

* Prepare as much of the meal as you can during the slow time of your day and when you are most refreshed. (This is very important.)

* Slow cook meats in the oven or in a crock pot.

* Keep your kitchen clean so you have an uncluttered work area.

Here are some ideas on what to prepare. These aren't elaborate gourmet meals. If you are too busy to cook dinner, then you are to busy to make gourmet dinners. Stick with the basics and keep it simple like our grandmothers did.

Roast: Place a roast in a crock pot or pan. Peel five potatoes and carrots and drop them in with it and turn on the oven. This takes five minutes. Clean and cut broccoli, celery and cucumbers for a salad -- five minutes. At dinner time, chop lettuce and tomato for the salad, adding the already prepared veggies. Then put the meat and the fixings on a platter -- five more minutes. Voila! Dinner in 15 minutes.

Stew: It takes me seven minutes to cube meat, peel five potatoes, carrots and onions, toss it into a pot and to season it. At dinner time, I put bread or dinner rolls on the table -- one to two minutes and I have dinner in nine minutes.

Ask your butcher to cube or slice all your meat for you. They usually charge nothing or just a few cents per pound. It saves not only time in cutting but in clean up too.

Chicken: Toss a chicken in a pan or crock pot -- two minutes. Clean potatoes to put in with chicken or to bake in the oven -- three minutes. At dinner time, warm a veggie -- two minutes. Slice some fruit -- three minutes. Dinner in 10 minutes.

Lasagna: Put noodles in a pot to boil -- one minute. Fry hamburger, get out cheese, tomato sauce and the rest of the fixings; mix sauce while noodles boil, 7-8 minutes. Layer everything -- two minutes. Cover and put in the fridge for dinner the next day or that evening. Put the lasagna in the oven to heat while getting out of your work clothes, checking the mail, etc. Set the table and cut a salad -- five minutes. Dinner is served; 15 minutes.

Beef stroganoff: Make your beef stroganoff in your crock pot. (If you don't want to use a crock pot, this recipe usually takes very little time just stirring it up in a pan.) Dump everything but sour cream and noodles, into the crock pot -- three minutes and simmer all day on low. Clean carrots, celery sticks and broccoli for a relish dish (five minutes) and put it in the fridge. At dinner time, boil egg noodles (5-7 minutes). While they are boiling, add sour cream to sauce and set the table. Total time: 15 minutes.

Chili: Mix everything in a pot the night before. Depending what you put in, it should take 5-10 minutes. Simmer throughout the next day.

Soup: Do the same as with the chili.

These are just general example of ways to fix meals easily and quickly. It isn't really a matter of time as much as it is a matter of being organized and getting things done before you are too exhausted to think.

If you have meats thawed and the ingredients on hand, most things can be tossed together in about the same time as it takes to order and wait to get your food at a fast food place.

Also, remember when you have your oven going to try to cook more than one thing in it. For example, if you are going to be baking a casserole, bake a pan of brownies, muffins or baked apples at the same time.

UNANSWERED QUESTIONS

Why do croutons come in airtight packages? Aren't they just stale bread to begin with?

Time Saving Kitchen Tips

Make simple meals. One-dish meals can contain your meat, your vegetable and your bread.

Things to do the night before:

* Plan your meals.

* Put things in the refrigerator to defrost.

* Pack lunches.

* Set the table for breakfast. Prepare breakfast foods the night before. For pancakes, mix dry ingredients the previous night. In the morning, add wet ingredients and cook.

Cook Once, Cook Big:

* Make large batches of beans and store in 1- or 2-cup portions.

* Make large batches of granola and store in an airtight container. If used for lunches or snacks, divide into single-serving plastic bags or containers

* Brown a large portion of ground beef and store in 1-cup portions. You can also do this with roast, pork and round steak.

* Cut up extra ingredients for another meal when using onions, green peppers, etc.

* Cook double batches of rice or pasta to be reheated later in the week.

Buy staples that you use often in quantity.

Make double or triple the amount when you prepare main dishes. Freeze. Label with the name of the dish and cooking instructions. Later when you are too busy to cook, put in the crockpot on low or set the timer for the oven to start dinner before you get home.

Place all pre-made meals in one part of the freezer. That way your husband and kids can easily find the meals when you aren't at home.

Try exchanging meals with another family. Cook double the amount and take half over to them. Later, they cook double and bring it to you. That is one less night you have to cook and it brings variety to your menu.

Have family members help. There is no reason why the kids can't help out with the cleaning, including dishes and other chores, so that you have time to prepare meals. Have everyone remove his or her own dirty place setting from table and put away 4 or 5 additional items. The table will be cleared quickly using this method. Wash your dishes right away. If you don't let them sit, the food will not get stuck on them. This will save you a lot of time-- you have to clean the kitchen before the next meal.

When unloading the dishwasher, set the table for the next meal.

Put away containers and clean up as you cook.

HEALTHY DIET

The Federal Drug and Food Administration is planning to issue a guide for proper eating that advises you to:

A. List your ten favorite foods.

B. List your five favorite beverages.

C. List all green vegetables that look like marsh grass, fur balls, or little trees.

D. List water.

E. Avoid A & B; eat only C; drink only D.

Packing Food for Road Trips

Over the River and Through the Woods to Grandma's House We Go --
Again!

Hoooraaay!!!! It's summer. That means exciting vacations and special trips to Grandma and Grandpa's house! You have dreamed about it all winter long -- your family, together in the car laughing, singing and playing road trip games. You stop at delicious restaurants --you know, the kind you see on Oprah where they serve the best hamburger or pie in the world. It's totally relaxing. You finish your meal, savoring that last cup of coffee. You climb back in the car to complete the journey. Then you arrive at Grandma's !!!!!! (or Disneyland!!!!!) ..... Now wake up! --As I said, you were only dreaming.

Now it's time to take your real trip. After spending several grueling hours trying to fit ten suitcases into a four suitcase carrier top, you are finally ready to leave. Let the games begin! They (the games that is) usually start before you even get out of your driveway. Everyone drags to the car half asleep and grumpy. Then, there is the first fight of the day -- Who gets to sit where? Once you get that settled, you are on your way (or so you think). Two miles out of town, you learn that someone has forgotten to turn off the iron. You have no choice but to head back home. One hour later, you are once again cruising down the highway when you get to play the second game of the day -- the "bathroom game".

Child, "I have to go to the bathroom."

Dad "Didn't you go before we left home?"

Child, "Yes, but I have to go again."

Dad, "Well, you are going to have to hold it because there is no place to stop!"

Child, "But I really have to go. I can't wait another minute."

Dad, "Let me see if I can find a tree or a bush!" (Good luck trying to find a tree or bush if you are traveling across Kansas!)

80

Once you persuade the child to go to the bathroom standing between the open car doors, you forge on.

The next game takes a lot of skill and dexterity. It's called "Baby Diaper Blow Out". All at once, your older children start screaming "Oh! GROSS! Mommmmm!" You see them in the rear view mirror climbing on top of each other to get to the opposite side of the car from where the baby is sitting, grinning from ear to ear. You know you are in for big trouble.

About the time the odor reaches you, you KNOW you are in REALLY big trouble. Of course these games can only be played when the nearest town is at least an hour away. Once again, you pull over. Who gets to hold the poopy baby? Where will you put the poopy baby while cleaning him up? You can't use the back seat because it has diaper blow out shrapnel on it. To make it worse, mom tries to clean up the whole mess -- baby, car seat and sometimes the floor of the car, with only the few baby wipes that fit in that cute little container for your diaper bag. I think you can usually get 4 or 5 wipes in them. If all else fails, you can always dig out the extra wipes you packed in the suitcase that is tied on the top of the car in the too small carrier. Look at the bright side -- You could be doing all of this in a freezing snow storm instead 100 plus degree weather!

Half an hour later, everyone finally piles back into the car. This is not your idea of seeing America... After an hour's worth of driving, you hear the first "I'm hungry". You are more then willing to stop, if for no other reason then to find a place to trash that stinky diaper.

Next Decision: Since you are so far behind on your schedule, do you get it "to go" or do you stop and go inside to eat? If you go inside, you will have a battle on your hands trying to drag your three year old away from the McDonald's playground. That last thought scares you more then the idea of pop and ketchup stains in the car, so you start hitting the drive-thru windows. I made that plural because, of course, everyone wants something different to eat and this is, after all, everyone's vacation. Three restaurants later, you hit the highway.

Now comes the part of the trip you like the best. Everyone is full and tired, so they lay back and take a nap. You hunker down, ready to relax and enjoy the view. In one split second, you forget the view and your eyes rivet to the rear view mirror once again. "Mommmm! I'm going to be sick!"

I've never seen a mom move as fast as when she hears those dreaded words. The timing is impeccable. In one swift, single motion, off comes moms seatbelt. At the same time, she twists, turns and flips over the seat, grabbing junior by the neck and shoving his head out the window, all the while hoping that dad was on top of the game enough to have the window down for her. Another good save by mom!

Ten hours later, you arrive at your destination 200 miles from home. You haven't been this dirty, smelly or tired since your last vacation, but you are sure it is all worth it. (You're sure, right???)

I know a lot of you are thinking that you would love to be taking even a bad vacation right about now, but with gas prices so high you can't imagine that's possible. Here are some suggestions that might help you:

First, you don't necessarily have to leave town to take a vacation. I have spent some of my best vacations just staying at home. We would get up when we wanted, eat a couple of meals out at our favorite restaurants, read or watch TV all day or go on picnics. We just did what we wanted. If you have a little money, but not enough for gas, then check into a hotel in town and swim for a day or two. That's what most kids love to do anyway and, once you're inside, most hotels look pretty much the same whether you are in South Dakota or Texas.

If you have some money saved for a trip but you know that the gas cost is going to eat most of your funds, try cutting your budget in another area, like your food. Consider taking your food with you.

At first this may not seem to be as much fun but you might be surprised. I recently took two different trips with the grandkids. For one trip, we decided to stop for fast food meals along the way. We were getting tired and hungry. We exited off the highway and of course there was the great debate about which fast food place to stop. Once we finally decided that, we tried to find a parking place because half the population of the United States had chosen to stop at the same McDonald's as us. We dragged ourselves out of the car, grabbing kids' hands to keep them from becoming road kill under the tires of the cars rushing through the drive-thru. Once inside, we stood in line and stood in line and stood in line......Thirty minutes later, we had our food. The place was packed, but we finally found a booth where all of us could pack in together like we were in the car. One spilled pop and dumped order of fries later, we threw the half eaten remains of the food into the trash and hit the road again.

The next trip, we decided to pack our food. Not only did it save money, but it seemed much easier. We planned to stop at a park or rest area. While we were laying out the food the kids ran around like a bunch of wild things getting rid of much of their pent up energy. If there was a spill, it was no big deal because it was on the grass. There was very little food left over because I had packed foods that were special treats. We packed up the little food that remained and saved it for later. It was so much more fun sitting under the trees enjoying the breeze than sitting packed like sardines in a booth at a fast food place. Even on warm summer days, there is usually enough wind and shade to make it comfortable to sit outside.

Going out to eat on a trip does not hold the excitement that it once did. Most families go out to eat so often at home that the novelty of it has worn off. The next time you travel try packing your own food, not only to save money but also to experience something fun and different. You might even try half and half. Pack for one meal and eat out for another. And don't forget breakfast -- Sometimes getting on the road the first thing in the morning is such a rush that it might be easier to wait and eat breakfast after you have driven an hour or two. This works especially well if you have to start out in the wee hours of the morning.

If your budget allows it, pack foods that your family only gets for special occasions. Here are a few ideas to get you started:

Breakfast

* **Muffins,** banana or apple bread
    Don't forget the butter or cream cheese

* **Donuts,** honey buns
    If you think it will be easier for you, buy them individually packaged. I'm not sure why, but kids seem to love individually packaged things and it makes everything more fun.

* **Bagels** with cream cheese and jam
    Mix the jam and cream cheese together and place in a small container before you leave.

* **Individual boxes of cereal with milk**

When I was young I always thought that it was so neat to be able to cut the sides of the boxes open and use the cereal box for a bowl. My mom thought it was neat because she didn't have to bring extra bowls and could toss the boxes.

* Hard boiled eggs

* Little smoky sausages (the pre-cooked kind)
These can be eaten out of the package, but if you like them hot, place them in a small thermos and pour very hot to boiling water over them. Put on the lid and by the time you are ready to eat them, the water will have heated them through.

Lunch and Dinner

* Sandwiches
Sandwiches are always great for a trip. Use hoagie buns instead of regular sandwich bread. It makes them a little more special and they don't crush as easily.

Good old peanut butter is great for the kids. Pay just a few more pennies and get the peanut butter in the tube. No messy knives and it's smaller than a jar. If you have spare packets of jelly from eating out, use those or buy jelly in the tube, too.

If you put lettuce or tomato on your sandwiches, bag them separately and put them on just before you are ready to eat.

* Chicken or slices of ham
Fried chicken is always a good picnic stand by. See later tips on keeping it cold.

* Hot dogs
As with the little sausages, put the hot dogs in a thermos and cover with boiling water. They will be perfectly cooked when ready to eat. To me these are so much easier than sandwiches and everyone loves them.

* Potato salad or pasta salad
Keep them in a small cooler.

* Chips, crackers and cheeses
>Buy chips in the cans. Slice or cut cheeses into cubes before you leave. Cheese sticks are perfect.

* Baked beans
>Once again, they keep great in a thermos.

* Fruits and veggies
>Apples, Oranges (already peeled) and firmer fruits.
>Clean and bag carrot sticks, celery, broccoli, cauliflower or other vegetables.

* Cookies, brownies, quick breads and muffins
>These are the best desserts.

* Drinks
>Of course pop works great, but I like to freeze bottles of lemonade. Lemonade seems more refreshing. You can also have juice or iced tea in bottles and coffee in a thermos for coffee drinkers. Be sure to freeze all your drinks to help keep your other foods cool in place of ice.

Don't forget the water.

General Tips

* Kids usually whine and fuss for one of two reasons. They are hungry or tired. This is especially true on trips, so bring plenty of snacks and a pillow for everyone.

* If you have room, box each family member's meal in his own box like the box lunches they give out at activities. This is really handy if you have to eat while driving. When finished eating, each person can put his empty wrappers in his own box for easy clean up.

* Be sure to bring those extra ketchup, mustard, salt, and pepper packets you get from fast food. Don't forget the plastic knives, forks and spoons along with napkins and a paring knife. Make sure just about everything is disposable.

* If money is tight, you don't have to have elaborate meals. I still fondly remember the trips when we stopped and bought a bag of chips, a loaf of bread, a package of bologna and cheese. We washed it down with an icy cold Pepsi and nothing tasted better.

* If you can, buy the gadget that you plug into the lighter plug in your car to heat water. It works well for instant coffee, oatmeal and hot chocolate.

* In this day and age with so many convenience foods available, it isn't hard to pack a lunch for the road. Even using those convenience foods, it is usually cheaper than buying food for the whole family at a fast food place.

A father was at the beach with his children when the four-year-old son ran up to him, grabbed his hand, and led him to the shore where a seagull lay dead in the sand.

"Daddy, what happened to him?" the son asked. "He died and went to Heaven," the Dad replied. The boy thought a moment and then said, "Did God throw him back down?"

Cleaning Cents

Improve Your Life Right Away – Get Dressed!

Just getting yourself dressed can make your life better!

Do you want to get out of debt? Do you want to get your house organized and have more control over your life? Do you want your family to respect you more than they do? Then get dressed!

I realize that for some people, like those with newborns and toddlers, this can be a challenge to say the least, but do what you can. At first it may mean only getting dressed during the baby's first nap of the day, but keep working at it until you can comb your hair and put on your make-up.

Getting dressed may not seem important but it really is at the top of the list of things you can do to improve your life. I had a woman once tell me she never got dressed in the morning, but that she could do her housework just fine. This same woman in the next breath was bemoaning the fact she couldn't get her family to help her or show her any respect. Take a good long look in the mirror at yourself and see what your family sees. Is it a woman perpetually dressed in pajamas or sweats, with hair sticking out all over and without any make-up? I know they are your family and are supposed to love you no matter how you look. They would never ever say anything to you because they do love you, but there is a difference between love and respect.

I know several women who never ever put on make-up or get dressed unless they are going to work or out someplace fancy. How do you think that makes their husbands and children feel? The message that a family receives is that they are not as important as the rest of the world. Many of these women wonder why their families don't respect them! If your boss showed up each day to work in her pajamas, without make-up and combed hair and then proceeded to sit down at her cluttered desk before demanding that you keep your desk spotless, wear pantyhose and a skirt and keep your nails manicured, how would you feel? Would you respect her? Would you want to even introduce her to your friends? You might do what she says, but you wouldn't respect her.

Do you think your husband and young children don't notice how you present yourself? Do you remember as a young child seeing your mom all dressed up to go to church or out for the evening and being so proud of how beautiful she looked? If your mom never dressed up, do you remember seeing your friends moms and wishing yours looked like that? Children notice even the littlest things. One day, my 5 year old granddaughter hugged me and said "Nan, you and Great Grandma always smell so good!" Even something as small as using a little perfume makes an impression and leaves a lasting memory.

I'm sorry, but it's a fact of life you have to earn respect. The dictionary's definition for earn is "to receive something for work done." The definition of work is "sustained physical or mental effort to overcome obstacles and achieve an objective or result." Translated, that means to get respect you will have to put forth some effort -- sustained or continual effort, even when there are Legos -- um I mean "obstacles" in your path.

One time I had to have major surgery. It was complicated by the fact I had a chronic illness and I was just plain worn out. The doctor insisted that I get some major rest. She told me that I was not to get out of my pajamas for three weeks. Why? Because once I got dressed, it was a signal for my friends and family that I was up to working again. Sure enough, the minute I slipped my clothes on, they were all over me. Now you may be reading this story and saying "If that's the case, I'll never get dressed again!" Trust me, I was tempted to stay in my pajamas for the rest of my life. But the point I'm trying to make is the way that you dress does send a signal -- to your family and yourself.

If you have been neglecting this part of your life and have been frustrated with a general lack of cooperation from your family, could it be that you have been giving them mixed signals?

THOUGHT OF THE DAY

Tomorrow I'm going to stop procrastinating.

Are You Choosing a Dirty House?

Sometimes, we can cut down the amount of hours we spend cleaning by simply making wiser choice and changing our habits. Here are some examples to help you get your house in order.

A woman with four children under the age of six decides she wants beige carpet throughout her house. She then spends the next few years nagging her family to be careful. A portion of every day is spent cleaning spots off the carpet. Then she complains to a friend that her husband and children are slobs because they make a mess of her carpet every day.

The reality is that her family is unusually careful when it comes to making messes and if she had a twill type darker carpet with a small pattern you wouldn't be able to see any spots.

A friend of my daughter's was complaining about how many loads of wash she had to do every day for her small family. When my daughter suggested that she have her family wear the same pair of jeans a second time if they were clean, her friend became angry at the very thought.

The reality is that if clothes still appear clean and don't smell, there is no harm in wearing them again. I have never heard of anyone dying or getting some exotic disease from wearing their jeans a second or third time or even for a week, but I have known of children who have been needlessly mistreated by grumpy, angry and overworked moms.

Do you insist that everyone get a clean towel every time he takes a bath? Why? Assign each person a towel and have him use it two or three times. When you get out of the bath, your body has just been scrubbed down and cleaned (we hope!). You're getting less dirt and germs on that towel than you are on the sheets that you have slept on for a week or more.

One interesting observation about people who are obsessive about one use washing: It's not really about the dirt. I have noticed that women who insist on washing everything after one use often allow their children to wear their winter coats and tennis shoes until they are so grungy that you aren't sure what color they once were.

We knew a woman whose children would come in from their swimming pool every day all summer long and drip pool water on her good hardwood floors. Each time it happened (several times a day), she would scold them and then mop up the floor. The bathroom where the children changed out of their swim suits was against an exterior wall right next to the back yard patio. The reality was that for a small amount of money-- which this family could easily afford, she could have put a door leading from the pool to the tiled bathroom, but she refused to have it done because she insisted that they learn not to walk inside while dripping.

In case you think I exclude my own habits, I too have had this problem. I used to iron everything. With my first child, I even ironed my baby's little t-shirts and pajamas. When my second baby came, he had very bad colic followed by pneumonia. (It took many weeks and four pediatricians to find out what was wrong.) I had walking pneumonia for three months, but I was still trying to iron everything. There were days I would only get up long enough to take care of the kids and then would collapse on the floor because I didn't have the strength to make it to bed. Well, one day a little light bulb went off in my head-- Maybe I should stop ironing (at least for this season in my life). Duh!

Don't get me wrong-- If having beige or white carpet inspires you to clean, puts a song in your heart and gives you warm fuzzies then by all means choose the beige carpet. Carpet your walls if it makes you feel that good. The same goes with the laundry. If it fills your heart with pride to see your children in freshly washed clothes, then let them change their clothes every hour.

The easiest way to keep your sanity is to reduce the things you do to the simplest process that gets the job done. If you want to be especially picky about one thing and you don't mind spending the extra time, go ahead and do it. Just don't neglect maintaining your home by becoming obsessed with it and, most importantly, do not blame your family for the extra work it causes you. It is not fair to them for you to take your anger out on them because you choose to do more work than necessary.

There is a verse in the Bible that says "Every wise woman builds her house, but the foolish one tears it down with her own hands." (Proverbs 14:1) Measure everything you say and do by asking yourself this question:

"Is it going to be for the good of my family and build it up or is it just the way I want things done even if it tears down my family?"

Here are some quick tips to start saving time and energy by changing habits:

* If clothes are clean, hang them up and wear them again.

* Spot clean clothes - If they have just one dirty spot, take a wash rag and wash it off. Then wear it again.

* Let each family member use one towel per week.

* When remodeling or replacing items, get things that will make cleaning easier. Get carpet that will conceal dirt. Don't put in tile -- The grout is horrible to clean.

* Put down inexpensive throw rugs under tables if a vinyl floor is not possible in the dining area.

* Allow the family to eat only at the table to avoid food messes in the rest of the house.

* Make toddlers wear a bib or oversized t-shirt when eating.

* Serve only light colored drinks if you have light colored carpet such as white grape juice, lemonade and of course water.

* Don't overdo when buying clothes. A four week supply of clothes isn't necessary for every member of the family. Ten days worth of clothing is plenty for most people. Unless you work outside the home, five dresses for church, two pairs of jeans, two pairs of dress pants and some blouses are more than enough.

* Buy clothes that don't need to be taken to the dry cleaners.

* Don't clean if it doesn't need it. Who says you have to vacuum everything every week? For a seldom used room like a guest room, don't waste time vacuuming it every week.

* Don't dust until you see dust.

* If there is something that continually frustrates you, fix it. If you can't find you keys, put a nail in the wall and them by the door. Put them there as soon as you walk in and you will know right where they are when you leave. If the door knob doesn't work properly, fix it. Sometimes we think that we are too busy to take care of these things, but eventually the hassle of working around something exceeds the time necessary to fix it. It literally takes thirty seconds to pound a nail into the wall to solve a chronic problem. I once heard someone refer to this as being "too busy driving to stop for gas". Just do it!

Top Ten Sayings of Biblical Mothers

10. Samson! Get your hand out of that lion. You don't know where it's been! (Judges 14:5-8)

9. David! I told you not to play in the house with that sling! Go practice your harp. We pay good money for those lessons!

8. Abraham! Stop wandering around the countryside and get home for supper!

7. Shadrach, Meshach and Abednego! Leave those clothes outside, you smell like a dirty ol' furnace!

6. Cain! Get off your brother! You're going to kill him some day!

5. Noah! No, you can't keep them! I told you, don't bring home any more strays!

4. Gideon! Have you been hiding in that wine press again? Look at your clothes! (Judges 6:11)

3. James and John! No more burping contests at the dinner table, please. People are going to call you the sons of thunder! (Mark 3:17)

2. Judas! Have you been in my purse again?

1. Moses, Quit setting fire to the bushes!

Dirty Dishes Cause Debt

The most common question that people ask me is "Where do I start to get out of debt?" After telling me of her huge credit card debt and how they eat out almost every night, the lady took a deep breath and said, "How do I save on laundry detergent and cleaning supplies?" Sometimes we can't see the forest for the trees. Even though saving money on cleaning supplies does help and should be done, that usually isn't where the biggest problem with the debt lies. This woman never once thought to ask me how to stop eating out so much. Most people don't want to face the real causes of their debt. Their biggest problems are the things they like the most. Going out to eat is one of the top five causes of debt.

Get those dirty dishes out of the sink!!

We go out to eat because we can't face a dirty kitchen. Keeping your kitchen empty of dirty dishes is the key to saving money. This is probably the #1 way to start getting out of debt. Most people are so overwhelmed with piled counter tops and dirty dishes that they would rather go out to eat than face a dirty kitchen. Do the dishes after every meal and keep hot soapy water in the sink while you are baking or cooking. Clean up as you go. If your sink is empty and the dishes are washed, your kitchen always looks good. This helps you save money because you have the time and space to cook.

To get in and out of the kitchen quickly, try these easy steps.
1. Put all dirty dishes in the dishwasher. Fill the sink with hot soapy water and put the hand washables in it to soak.
2. Wipe off counter tops and tables with hot soapy water. (This way, if you have unexpected company, at least your table and counters will be clean.)
3. Sweep the floor and shake throw rugs if needed.
4. Wash the dishes that have been soaking.
5. Wipe down the faucets and dry with a towel. (Be sure to wipe any sticky appliances, too.)
6. Put out a clean dishrag and towel.
7. Take out the trash.

These simple steps can help you start climbing your way out of debt. You will be amazed how much better you will feel just having the kitchen clean.

94

Clean and Organize in Five Minutes!

I always dreaded cleaning or organizing. I am not born organized so I have had to train myself to be organized. Often, my problem staying organized is that I think about the thing that needs to be done so much that I begin to dread it. Here are a few tips I used to change my attitude about the things I dreaded:

Time yourself to see how long it takes to do a chore.

Two days ago I cleaned the fridge. It took me two minutes to clean off one shelf. After a child meltdown, I came back and finished. It took me 10 minutes to clean the entire thing and that included three minutes cleaning up a mess from my two year old "helping" by dumping something on the floor.

I used to hate to make the bed. Then I timed myself. It takes me exactly 1 minute.

To clean-out my "plasticware" shelf, it took me five minutes.

To clean the bathroom sink and toilet, it took me five minutes including wiping down the floor. Adding the tub (removing the contents and cleaning) took another 5 minutes so it took only ten minutes to clean the entire thing!

It really doesn't take as long as you would think to get cleaned and organized. When you realize it only takes one minute or ten minutes to do something, it doesn't seem so bad!

Do one thing for five minutes and see how far you can get.

Identify the thing that is bugging you the most and do it first!

Often, we have lots of little things that need to be cleaned, repaired or organized, but we don't want to deal with them right now. Sometimes it pays to just make the time rather than to keep putting it off.

Our front door is mostly glass. The fingerprints on the front door were driving me crazy! While David was eating, instead of doing the dishes, I ran down and wiped the down the door. (It took 3 minutes.) It has been bugging me for days. As soon as I took the three minutes to do it, it was off my mind and I could go on and do the dishes.

I have always dreaded unloading the dishwasher. One day, I timed myself and it takes only three minutes. Keeping that in mind, it doesn't seem so bad.

Mike wanted to change the door knob on our front door. It didn't work correctly and we kept getting locked out. He bought a new door knob, but he was in the middle of another project and didn't change it right away. One day, after sidestepping it for a while, he decided to stop everything else and change it. It took five minutes. He said if he had known that's all the time it would take, he never would have waited so long to do it.

Most of the time we spend more time thinking about these things than just taking the time to do it and get it over with! Now walk away from the computer and take care of that thing that is bothering you! ;-)

"Cleanliness is not next to godliness.

It isn't even in the same neighborhood. No one has ever gotten a religious experience out of removing burned-on cheese from the grill of the toaster oven."

Erma Bombeck

Secrets of the Organized

1. Never stop picking up.

*Try picking up during TV commercials or while you are waiting for something to boil on the stove. You will be amazed how much you can get done in five minutes.

*Have the entire family spend five minutes picking up the family room or living room before they go to bed. Set a timer for young kids so they don't get overwhelmed.

*If your family members go to bed at different times then have each member pick up his or her items before bed time. Once this becomes a habit, you will be amazed how much easier picking up becomes.

2. Stop making messes.

*Keep a trash can in every room. No one likes carrying one small piece of trash from the family room to the kitchen so it usually ends up on the floor. Keep small trash cans everywhere. In our office we have two trash cans, one next to the desk for throwing away regular office trash and one next to the shipping table for throwing away envelope tabs, extra invoices and other shipping trash. If you need two trash cans in a room put them in there. Make it easy to keep things clean.

*Throw that sticky food wrapper straight into the trash. Don't lay it on the counter to make another mess that needs to be wiped up later.

* Don't lay that dirty spoon on the counter. Rinse it and put it in the sink or dishwasher.

*As you're undressing, don't throw your dirty clothes on the floor or on the furniture. While they are still in your hand, put them in the hamper or if they're still clean, hang them up. (A hamper without a lid works best.)

*Keep the hamper close to where you undress at night. If it is convenient, you will be more likely to use it.

*Before you leave the bathroom, hang your wet towel on the rod. Don't drop it on the floor or leave it in a pile.

3. Think ahead.

*What are you having for dinner?

*Are the kid's papers signed and ready for school?

*What clothes are you wearing tomorrow?

4. Never, Never Procrastinate.

*Keep straightening things all the time. For example, when you put away groceries and you see that the cans of soup have fallen over, take two seconds to restack them.

*When you put linens or clothes in their drawers, make sure everything in those drawers is neatly stacked.

*Pick up as you go. Each time you walk through a room, pick up something.

*Stop thinking about it! Just do it.

5. Don't give up. Practice makes perfect.

*Train family members to rinse their own dishes and stack them in the sink (or better yet to put them directly into the dishwasher). It may take a while to develop this habit. For kids, you may want to do something like charge each member a dime for every dish not rinsed or make them responsible for doing all the dishes for a week.

*Remember Thomas Edison? What if he had given up after his first 5, 10, or 100 light bulbs? Where would we be now if he had thrown up his hands and quit at his first failures? The same is true with getting and staying organized. Keep practicing and you will create a productive new habit.

6. Attitude, Attitude, Attitude.

*Stop dreading taking care of your home and start taking pride and
pleasure in it. Think of an organized home as a special gift of peace and
pleasure that you are giving your family. A disorganized one causes
turmoil and frustration. Besides -- You probably spend more time
worrying about it than it would take to clean it.

7. Use rooms for their intended purposes.

*Don't let kids get undressed in the family room - that's why they have
bedrooms.

*Eat food at the kitchen table or bar, not in bed. This alone can save a
huge number of messes.

*Fold laundry in the laundry room immediately after taking it out of the
dryer and put it away immediately.

8. Be a wise steward of your time.

*If you see something that needs to be clean, clean it as soon as possible.

*If something doesn't need to be cleaned, don't waste your time. If there is
no dust, don't just dust because you dust every Saturday.

*Don't overbook yourself volunteering at schools, churches or charities.
Learn to say "no". Notice that I didn't say don't do these things at all, just
control how much you do so they don't take over your life.

* Don't overbook your children with their activities, either.

*Get rid of fruitless activities. Many of us spend way too much time talking
on the phone, watching TV, shopping unnecessarily or killing time on the
computer. These are all time robbers when you devote a lot of time to
them.

9. Keep on top of things.

*If you do small cleanings every day, you'd be surprised how much you can accomplish. In ten minute increments, you can do each of the following: wash the dishes, vacuum, file a pile of papers or clean your purse. It shouldn't take more than ten minutes for each child to pick up his room before bed and to lay out his clothes for the morning.

*Don't let the laundry, dishes, toys and paperwork get out of control.

THIS IS MOTIVATION TO GET IT CLEANED UP!

In January 2006 a woman in Shelton, Washington, who had been reported missing was found dead under a large pile of debris in her house. According to news reports and interviews with police, the woman apparently suffocated under a giant mound of clutter.

The local police chief said, "In some areas, clothes and debris were piled 6 feet high."

To give you an idea of the extent of the clutter, it took police officers 10 hours of searching to find the woman.

The next time you're having trouble motivating yourself, think about this story and grab a box of trash bags…

How To Stay Organized And
Save Money

Don't procrastinate!

If you leave it today for tomorrow you will still have to do it, so just do it now and get it off your mind.

Pay your bills on a regular basis.

Twice a month or once a week. When a bill comes in the mail open it immediately. Keep all your bills in one place with pens, pencils with working erasers, calculator, envelopes, and postage stamps.

If you are unable to pay a bill.

Call the place to whom it is owed BEFORE it is due. Explain your situation and see if you can work out a payment plan. Most places would be more than happy to work out a payment plan rather than not receive the money or have to call a collection agency.

Keep a master to-do and to-call list.

I keep a small spiral notebook. I divide each page in half with a line and everyday I write down what needs to be done. One side of the line is for the "To Do" items and the other side is for "To Call" items. If you like you can use one page for each day. If you need to do something on Wednesday and it's Monday, write it on your to-do list for Wednesday.

Look at your list from a priority standpoint.

What needs to be done first? Number items on your list according to their importance starting from 1 and then work on the most important things first.

Don't over schedule yourself.

Be flexible and allow yourself some room for illness, unexpected appointments etc.

For appointments...

Always plan to be early and bring something to do (like a magazine or novel you want to read). Make sure that you bring something along for the kids also.

Keep a master list of weekly housecleaning duties and assign a day for them to get done.

If you clean the bathrooms every Monday, you don't have to worry about wondering when they were last cleaned.

Create a place for items waiting to leave the house.

Create a place, preferably by the door, in the house for everything that needs to be returned, including library books, dry cleaning, letters to be mailed, etc. Then you won't have to search for things when you are leaving.

Put the children to bed at least 1 hour before your bed time.

Use the time to relax and get things done that would be easier and faster to do without their "help". There is no reason that the kids need to be up late and the quiet time will reduce your stress level.

Try waking up 15 minutes earlier each morning.

This gives you a little breathing time before you have to start hurrying for the day. Take time to enjoy your cup of coffee.

Children want quantity time not quality time.

They can help you with the lawn work, dishes, laundry, dusting, vacuuming and other household chores. They will learn the things they need for life while spending time with mom and dad.

Make your kitchen utensils accessible.

Put frequently used kitchen items like ladles, wooden spoons and spatulas in a container on the counter near the stove. It frees up storage space and makes them easier to access.

Cut knives from your silverware drawer (pun intended ;-).

Instead of storing knives in a drawer, try putting them on a rack on the wall.

Store linens in the rooms where they are used.

Try different storage areas. For example, store kitchen linens on a cabinet shelf instead of stuffed in a drawer.

There's never time to put it away,
but there is always time to look for it.

One particular four-year-old prayed, "And forgive us our trash baskets as we forgive those who put trash in our baskets."

The Basics of Tossing!

At times, all of us spend money on items that we don't end up using. For most of us, we spend a lot of money on these things. For some of us, it is exercise equipment; for others it might be clothes, toys, kitchen gadgets or tools. We keep them because we would feel guilty if we got rid of them. "I mean, Do you know how much that is worth?" or "What if I get rid of it only to discover that I need it?"

Why are you punishing yourself by keeping something that is cluttering your life? Stress is one of the biggest problems that Americans face today and disorganization and clutter are among the biggest causes of stress. If you bought something you don't use, face it. You made a mistake. Don't make an even bigger one by keeping it. Get rid of it and move on. Donate it to someone who can use it and relieve you and your family of the stress of living with it. Learn from your mistakes and try to evaluate better whether you actually need something before you spend money.

If you are saying, "...but that might be worth something", why don't you find out. If you are afraid to lose out on a financial windfall, sell it on Ebay or put it out for a garage sale. If you make big bucks, put it in the bank! If that item doesn't get $5.00 on Ebay, you probably overestimated its value. Toss it!

But what if you get rid of it and later find out that you do need it? Most of us save all sorts of things that we might use one day. Very few of us will ever use more than one thing in twenty that we keep "just in case". Think about this: If you sell the things that will put money in the bank, give the useful things you don't need to other people or a thrift store and toss the rest, you can't really lose. When you find out later that you needed that extra toolbox, take the money you made selling all the other stuff you never ended up needing and buy it! Almost everyone will be way ahead financially doing this because we will never need most of it. Not only that, but doing this will also eliminate the stress and expense of storing and moving it.

Oh and if it's trash but you feel guilty about separating yourself emotionally from it, just put it in the trash. Don't make the thrift store do it. Say a prayer over it if it makes you feel better and let it go.
Here are some specific things to work on:

1. **Do you have more than one of some utility item?** Keep your favorite or best and toss the rest. Many people keep four potato peelers, three strainers and five 9x13 pans. If this is you, do you often prepare meals for 50 or more people? No? Toss it!

2. **Food stuff -** Wow, food is a big one. I think it's because we think of all those starving people in some third world country. If you don't need it (unless you are ready to box it up and send it to them), toss it.

   If there are bugs on food items, if cans are swollen, or if items are past the expiration dates, then toss them. Staring at them every time you open the pantry isn't going to cure botulism.

   If you have more items then your family can eat in a year then use them before you buy more or donate them to a food bank. If you want to use it, but didn't realize you have 17 cans of beets and 12 cans of pie filling, you need a better pantry organization system.

3. **Are you really ever going to make that craft or sewing project?** Toss it.

4. **Why save 25 empty mayo jars when you only use two a year?**

5. **If you are saving a magazine that is dated from the last millennium** or even last year and haven't read it do you honestly think you're going to ever read it? Those hair styles aren't popular anymore and not many people even remember Commodore 64 computers.

6. **The same goes for newspapers.** If you didn't get yesterday's paper read, what makes you think you are going to read last week's? Time marches on and collecting newspapers can get you in hot water with the fire marshal.

7. **Why are you keeping it if it is torn, stained, too small or outdated?** Get rid of it. The moth balls just make your house smell funny.

8. How many tee shirts can you wear in a week? Why do you have 30 stuffed in your closet? How about pants, dresses, and pajamas?

9. Do I really need 5 pairs of brown loafers? Enough said.

10. Do your children play with the same half dozen favorite toys every day while the rest lay buried in the toy chest? Why are you saving the rest? Toss them! (But not in front of the kids. They will never consent to giving up anything!) If there are things they don't play with but you think they still like, put them in a box for a few months and trade them out with some of the other stuff when they get bored with what they have. Don't be a pack rat. If you have 12 boxes like this, keep tossing.

11. Do you really think that when your son is 35 years old, he will get a thrill out of looking at every school paper he ever did, especially the ones where he wrote the letter "D" a hundred and one times? Keep the highlights if you like, but if it takes more than a small box, keep tossing. Let's not even talk about saving every school paper you ever did for your kids.

The next time you open a closet and experience a major cave in, remember that stuff is not more important than your family. Your family deserves a peaceful, stress-free house and so do you. Are you choosing stuff over your family's well being? Ask yourself that question as you sort through your "things".

THOUGHT OF THE DAY

Junk is something you've kept for years and throw away three weeks before you need it

---

How Can I Get My Kids To Help?

"How can I get my kids to help?!" scream the mothers of the world! In all the years I have been a mother, almost every bit of advice I have studied say to motivate your kids using charts with stickers, allowances and various forms of bribery. I have personally used all of these methods. I believe in using them because I have found they work great.

Guess what? These methods work for teens too. When my son started high school, we got rid of the charts. We thought, "OK, he's growing up. He doesn't need them anymore." I spent a year reminding him five times a day to take out the trash. I'm not sure what I was thinking but I somehow got it in my head that when a person does the same chore every day for ten years, he might figure out that he will have to do it again tomorrow. Wrong!

At that time, I didn't know that the section of a teenaged boys brain that recognizes tasks that need to be done and motivates him to actually take action to complete those tasks doesn't really develop until he gets married or at least leaves home. If you have a teenager, once this happens, you will be surprised when you walk into the kitchen and discover a strange young man taking out your trash, even though it's not full and overflowing! He hasn't even been told to do it! So be encouraged -- there is hope!

Back to when he was still a teenager -- I did finally discover that if I wrote down a list of things that I needed done, my son responded much better to the list than he had responded to my continual nagging.

What kind of boss are you?

Just like in any business, the employees are only as good as the mangers are. Maybe we need to stop putting all the blame on our families and reflect on what kind of "bosses" we are.

There are certain places of business where I go and I can tell right away that they are great places to work. The merchandise is neatly displayed, the employees are smiling and laughing with each other and the customer service is wonderful. The employees seem to bend over backwards help the customers. What's the secret? They have a great boss.

Here is a list of characteristics of ineffective bosses and a effective bosses. Which one are you?

Ineffective Mom:

  * Barks orders
  * Yells
  * Criticizes everything, even when people have tried their best
  * Makes family feel guilty - No matter what they do, it's never enough.
  * Never happy with how the job is done
  * Tasks must be done the Mom's way and no other way. Mom will not even listen to reasonable suggestions.

Effective Mom:

  * Makes charts or lists, so the family knows what is expected
  * Makes requests in a quiet, gentle, reasonable voice with a smile
  * Always praises them for doing a good job or at least for trying
  * Shows her family how much she appreciates them for all they do to help her
  * Never fixes a job done less than perfectly. Instead, the next time the job is done, she does it with them until they lean to do it right.

Your husband and children are people with brains and good ideas. Make this a group effort and not a dictatorship. Every member of the family wants to feel needed and to be considered an important contributing member of the family.

The hardest part for you is that you need to take the time and trouble to train your children. Don't you hate starting a new job where you have had little or no training? You get so confused and frustrated that you just want to give up and quit. It can be that way with your family, too.

Many times, families quit on you because they don't understand what you expect from them, they don't know how to do a task or they can't seem to do it well enough for you. It may take several times to master a task (It may even take years), but keep working with your children until they feel comfortable with a job and you will help them develop into responsible, thoughtful adults. Always remember that a word of encouragement, a thank you, and a reward goes a long way.

Use a Dresser to Organize
Your Garage!

It seems like organizing your garage can be a never ending task. Lots of companies make millions of dollars selling all kinds of storage systems to try to make your garage just a little bit more organized. OK I'm about to confess -- We've had this problem, too! I know, it's hard to believe, isn't it? The cool thing is we found a great organization tool that cost us nothing...

We have a dresser that was given to us by a relative. It's an old 1970's style dresser with nine drawers. It is about three feet tall, eight feet wide and two feet deep. It was one of those pieces of furniture that makes one wonder, "Why would anyone ever have bought that?" It had the faux wood countertop on top and the drawer faces were covered with those really tacky twirly relief patterns people really liked in the 70's. Still, much to my husband's surprise, I could see the value in it!

I painted it black (except for the wood top) and then put in the garage to store stuff. Even my husband has been surprised to see how well it has worked out for us. Here's what I did:

First, I designated each drawer as a place for one category of supplies, and I marked each drawer with a little index card that I stapled to the front of the drawer with a staple gun.

One drawer is for electrical items. This includes outlets, outlet covers, electrical testing equipment, wire crimpers, lamp pieces and any other electrical thing we are likely to use. (Just as with any organizing, don't save stuff you'll never use just because you can ;-)

We have a drawer for paint supplies: roller handles, paint brushes, sand paper and such. (We don't keep paint there -- We have a separate small plastic shelf unit with our stash of paint.)

The top left drawer is our nail and screw drawer. We have two plastic embroidery floss organizers, each with twenty or so slots. We use one organizer for nails and the other for screws. When both of these containers are in the drawer, there is room for a few whole boxes of the nails and screws we use most often.

We seem to have problems with cords, so one drawer is just for cords. It includes a few lamp cords, cable wire, phone wire and other cords. I make each one into a coil and slide it into a toilet paper roll to keep it separate from the others. My husband likes to just wind each one up and wrap it like a noose.

There is a drawer that includes nothing but batteries, one for glues and adhesives and another dedicated exclusively to light bulbs.

Another drawer is for miscellaneous hardware. This is the drawer for felt chair legs, baby locks, door stops and all kinds of other items that don't have homes in any of the other drawers.

We also have one drawer set aside for miscellaneous tools. This drawer is for those tools that we don't use every day, but that come in handy every now and then. We use it for things like pipe wrenches, channel locks, a wire brush and extra socket sets.

On top of the dresser, I placed several small rectangular plastic containers the size of shoe boxes. One has hammers and such, one has screwdrivers, one has pliers and crescent wrenches. I have four or five of these all together. Essentially, they contain the tools we use most often. This arrangement also leaves us a little counter space on the dresser.

Using an old dresser for this purpose has made life so easy! I see them all the time at garage sales for $10. This is well worth the price for the amount of storage you can get and if you like to find new uses for things that otherwise might hit the landfill, an old dresser might just do the trick!

Think outside the box!

Dear Readers: We received this reader response after this story first appeared:

I recently saw your " Use a Dresser to Organize Your Garage!" article (from Living on a Dime) on The Dollar Stretcher, and I just had to laugh because I believe I own your dresser's little brother. It is a horrific, brown, 8' wide, 1.5' deep, billion-pound monstrosity with eight drawers that are so shallow that you cannot fit two stacked sweatshirts inside. My mother-in-law is to blame.

We have considered getting rid of it many times, particularly when we had last moved. However, at the same time, I was struggling to find space for all of my cookware, bakeware, and servingware; I do a great deal of cooking and baking, but my apartment kitchen is small and has very few cabinets. I had hoped to find an armoire-type cabinet to house it all, but even the unaffordable pieces weren't deep enough to accommodate most of my pans and large dishes and platters.

And then I had a brainstorm. I pushed the monstrosity against the wall of the dining room area (a feat in itself), filled the drawers with shallow pots, pans, baking sheets, muffin tins, serving dishes, etc, separating stacked items with bubble wrap, and covered the top with a long silk scarf and seasonal candles. It's not quite as elegant as a traditional "server," but it's camouflaged well enough that people generally ignore it, and it will serve us at least until we are able to save enough to buy a house. Maybe some day I will even paint it.

It's nice to know that I'm not the only person in the world who has given new life to an inherited monstrosity.
KMW

UNANSWERED QUESTIONS

Why do people keep running over a string a dozen times with their vacuum cleaner, then reach down, pick it up, examine it, then put it down to give the vacuum one more chance?

Save Money On Clothing

It's that time of year when everyone is thinking about fall wardrobes or kids' back to school clothes. We get so many questions about how to save on groceries but very few about how to save on clothes, even though many people spend two or three times as much per month on clothes than they do on their groceries.

I was talking to a woman recently who was bemoaning the fact she had just lost her job and didn't know what she was going to do for medical insurance. Then she started talking about how much she loved her clothes and couldn't give up buying them. She had a large collection of shoes, purses and tops. She owned over 150 pairs of pants. It hadn't even dawned on her that if she had taken the money she had spent on all those clothes she could have easily paid for many years worth of insurance.

It's time we start rethinking our clothing budgets. Try these tips to save some money on your clothing budget:

1. Stop shopping for clothes because of the "high" it gives you. When you use shopping as a drug, you no longer think rationally about how much money you're spending.

2. Stop shopping for clothes because it builds your self esteem. Yes, clothes do make us feel good about ourselves and there is nothing wrong with that, but you don't need 150 pairs of pants to do that. Shopping for self esteem is trying to fix an emotional problem with a physical solution and that will get you nowhere. That makes as much sense as discovering that your car ran out of gas and trying to solve the problem by washing it to try and make it run again. You're working on the wrong problem.

3. Plan your family's wardrobes. Don't just buy a cute top and take it home hoping you'll find something to go with it. If you need a suit jacket, get one you can wear to the office or that you can wear casually with jeans. Do you really need five pairs of black pants? Instead of buying another pair of black pants, why not buy a white blouse that will go with that pair of pants and skirt that you already have but that don't match anything else?

4. Basic sewing is easier than you think. Take care of the clothes that you do have:

* If things aren't dirty, wear them again. The less you wash things the longer they last. (Of course I don't mean underwear.)

* Hang up the clothes you can wear again when you take them off. So many kids and adults just drop their clothes on the floor when they take them off and later throw them in the laundry so they don't have to hang them up. Not only does this cause you twice as much work, It puts unnecessary wear and tear on your clothes.

* Don't get rid of that shirt because it is missing a button. Don't throw out your daughters jeans because they have a hole. Take two minutes to sew a button on the shirt or an appliqué on the jeans. (Yes, it really does take two minutes to sew on a button. Time yourself next time. You'll be surprised.)

5. Use the clothes you do have well. If jeans have a hole that can't be fixed then have the kids wear them for play clothes or cut them off for shorts. If that dress of yours is getting outdated, take out the shoulder pads or add shoulder pads (depending on the style),or take up or let down the hem. Update your outfits with different accessories.

6. Hang clothes on the line or rack to dry when possible. Dryers create a lot more wear and tear on the fabrics and usually destroy all elastic.

I do live in the real world and know that most people, like me, love clothes so I'm not saying don't ever buy anything new. If you're serious about controlling your spending or reducing debt then don't let your clothes shopping get out of control.

Remember: Stop buying clothes to satisfy your emotional needs. This will save you not only money, but also time, energy and the stress of taking care of all the clutter those extra clothes will cause.

Additional Tips from Readers To Make Your Clothes Last Longer:

* If you are having a hard time removing the stains around collars and cuffs, try using abrasive hand cleaner or shampoo.

* When dealing with stains, try using the same product on your clothes that you use to clean the part of your body adjacent to the stain. For example, use shampoo to remove collar stains, use your face cleanser to remove make up stains or use the soap that your husband uses on his hands after working on the car to remove grease and oil. Of course always spot test everything first so that you don't ruin the garment with the cleaner.

Real Mothers Know:

That their kitchen utensils are probably in the sandbox.

That dried play dough doesn't come out of pile carpet.

Don't want to know what the vacuum just sucked up.

God created company so the house would get cleaned.

Demystifying the Great Laundry Detergent Dilemma

I grabbed the phone and answered it. It was my daughter chuckling on the other end. "We got another one," she said, "Another laundry detergent e-mail." For years now we have one reoccurring question. How can I save on my laundry detergent?

This may seem like an innocent enough question, but when we find out the writer's story, laundry detergent is almost never really relevant to the problem. What we've found is that a person who asks about laundry detergent is usually on the brink of bankruptcy, divorce, or losing a job. It's like some kind of code word or distress signal for "Help Me -- I'm drowning in debt".

Often these people have maxed out their credit cards, have fully mortgaged a quarter of a million dollar home and owe money on several expensive new cars. They have closets full designer clothes, purses and shoes and say " How can I save on laundry detergent?"

For a person in this situation, asking that question makes as much sense as saying, "My home is burning down -- I must go back in and save that $3 carton of milk I bought today!" If it were me, I would say, " Forget the milk I going to save the family heirlooms, my gold jewelry and the good silver."

I have tried to understand why in a financial crisis so many people want to learn how to save money on laundry detergent when there are so many more obvious ways they could be saving. Here is what I have finally concluded:

First, by focusing on a trivial issue they don't have to look at the real, more serious problem. It's like putting a Band-Aid on a scratch on your finger while you are bleeding profusely from an artery on your leg. They don't want to acknowledge the real spending problem because then they would have to deal with it.

If you are in this situation and you want to be free of it, YOU HAVE TO ADMIT THERE IS A PROBLEM. You are spending more money then you make. It is important to realize that spending impulsively beyond your means is almost as bad as doing drugs. You get instant gratification and pleasure but over the long haul, it will destroy you.

Second, saving on laundry detergent gets rid of that nagging guilt for a little while. As long as they keep trying to save pennies on unimportant things, they don't have to feel guilty about spending thousands on the fun things. The problem is that if they are spending beyond their means, it will catch up with them eventually, which will make the stress and damage all the worse.

For those of you who have your finances under control and really do need a way to spend less on detergent, here are a few suggestions. At first I wondered how I could help anyone save money on detergent when a person uses so little of it? For a family of four, a 40-load box of detergent would last me one to two months, which doesn't give a lot to save on. It isn't the laundry detergent that people need to save on but the amount of laundry they are doing. It's seems as if people's laundry has turned into some kind of monster that is taking over their homes. It's everywhere. Piles of it on the floor, chairs, tables, and beds. Almost every horizontal surface in the house is covered with laundry -- dirty laundry, clean laundry and folded laundry.

By cutting back on the amount of laundry you do, you can save quite a bit on detergent, dryer sheets, fabric softener and hot water.

Here are a few ways to help you cut back:

* **Have the kids wear the same pair of pajamas every night.** Before you get upset and say there is no way you would allow them to do that think about this: You bathe your kids before they go to bed so their pajamas go on a clean body. How dirty could those pajamas get while they are sleeping? Most people don't change their sheets more than once a week. What is the difference between sleeping on the same sheets and sleeping in the same pajamas?

* **Assign each person his or her own towel** to use a minimum of two to three times instead of just once. In the case of young children let them use the same towel. Up to a certain age most people toss their little ones

all in the bath together so if they can share the same bath water they can share the same towel.

* **When you get home from church** or someplace where you didn't wear the outfit all day, change out of your good clothes and hang them up to wear again.

* **If it doesn't look dirty and doesn't stink, don't wash it.** We usually use jeans for a week at our house.

* **Don't be lazy.** So often we get undressed and, instead of putting our clothes away, we throw them on the floor in a heap. We don't want to iron, fold or even hang them up, so we just throw them in the wash. This makes more work later because we still have to iron, fold and hang them on wash day, but we also use more detergent, dryer sheets, fabric softener, hot water and time.

COMMERCIAL REWARD

At breakfast one day, I eagerly waited for John to comment on my first attempt at homemade cinnamon rolls.

After several minutes with no reaction, I asked, "If I baked these commercially, how much do you think I could get for one of them?"

Without looking up from his newspaper John replied, "About 10 years."

Air Drying Clothes
Without A Clothesline

We all know that if we don't dry our clothes in the dryer we save on electricity, but many of us don't think about how the dryer reduces the life of our clothes. For a long time I couldn't understand why so many people were buying scads of socks and underwear for their families every few months. When my children were growing up, they almost never wore out their underwear and socks and we owned only about a quarter as many pair as most people. No I didn't buy some name brand known for its child proof quality. I usually bought the least expensive ones I could find.

Fast forward a couple decades. One day after folding my grandson's new underwear, I noticed that the waistband was terribly rippled. After doing some research, I discovered the answer: The dryer was destroying the rubber elastic in the socks and underwear. I rarely dried my family's clothes in the dryer, so the elastic never broke down. It doesn't just happen with underwear - Have you ever noticed pilling (those little fabric balls) on your clothes and linens and the resulting lint in the dryer? That is the result of the fibers being rubbed thin. The dryer also shrinks clothes and sets in stains.

The two reasons I think most people don't line dry their clothes are that they think it is inconvenient or they're just not sure how to do it. Here are some of the best tips I have found to air dry clothes without a clothes line.

Though I don't use the dryer to dry my clothes, I do use it for five minutes or so with some loads (just long enough to fluff the clothes). I put one load in the dryer and only leave then there as long as it takes me to load the washer with the next load.

If you have no clothesline, you live in an apartment or your homeowners association won't allow clotheslines, here are a few ways to dry without a clothesline.

You need at least one drying rack and some type of clothes rod. You can buy drying racks at most discount stores or hardware stores. You might locate a clothes rod in your laundry room above the dryer, use a sturdy shower curtain rod in the bathroom or get a metal clothes racks that hooks over the back of a door. You don't need much. I can hang two loads of laundry on one drying rack and 2 feet of clothes rod.

Hanging on a Clothes Rod
Hang as many items as you can on clothes hangers, beginning with the obvious things like dresses, dress shirts and blouses and hang the hangers on a clothes rod to dry. Be sure not to put the hangers too close together or the clothes will not dry. You can also hang things like pajama tops, t-shirts, small kids shirts and one piece outfits. Lightweight pants, pajama bottoms, skirts and sweats can be pinned on clothes hangers and even sheets can be folded and hung on them. If you are really short of drying rack space, you can hang socks, underwear, wash rags, hand towels and towels on hangers and add them to your clothes rod, too.

Hanging on a Clothes Rack
When hanging clothes on a drying rack, I start at the bottom with socks and underwear, wash rags and baby clothes. Young children's clothes and hand towels go on the middle layer and the top rack is for towels, jeans, pillow cases, sweaters, sweats, pajama bottoms and t-shirts. I try to use every inch of space, so if I put a pillow case on the rack and there are a couple of inches left next to it I put a sock there. I even hook bras on the corners of the rack.

Drying racks are handy because they can be moved to speed up the drying process. Place them outside on a sunny (but not windy) day. Inside the house, try putting them over a vent and the heat or air conditioner will dry them faster. If you don't have central heat or air then you can place them in front of your heater or a fan. Don't place clothes close enough to heaters to be a fire hazard.

If you are short on space and don't want to look at a drying rack in the middle of the room, do the laundry before bed, hang it and in most cases it will be dry by morning (especially if you set it above an air vent).

Try hanging large king sized sheets or blankets over your shower rod, over the rail of your deck, between two lawn chairs or folded in half or quarters over your clothes rack. When you fold large items, you must flip and turn them every 5-10 hours so that each side gets dry.

Sometimes it is useful to hang a clothesline in the basement or attic. Be sure to check out your department stores and hardware stores for other ideas. They have many clever items like retractable clotheslines, things to hang over doors and some not so new ideas like extra large drying racks that can hold two loads of laundry each.

Even though this may sound complicated at first, once you do it a few times it becomes second nature to you. Pretty quickly, you will discover the most efficient way to hang your clothes on the rack. I know automatically that three wash rags fit across the bottom bar of my rack and the two socks will fit next the that particular t-shirt. It's like putting a puzzle together- the first time takes you longer than the times after that because you know where the pieces fit.

Thought Of The Day

No husband has ever been shot while doing the dishes

$40 Bedroom Makeover

By shopping at thrift stores and making do with what I had, I spent under $40 redecorating my daughter's room.

Elly's new room took me two days work, 15-30 minutes at a time, resting about 1-2 hours in between. It took me about one day to put the paint on the walls. (That's with the help of a 3 year old.) I was sick or I would have been able to complete it in one day.

To redecorate, we designed the room around a comforter that Elly had received from her grandmother as a gift. We purchased everything from the thrift store over 2 weeks. We had to go about 3-4 times, but it was well worth the savings.

For color on the wall behind the bed, I found a twin sheet that I had on hand that I had purchased for $1 at the thrift store. I ironed the sheet and then used the staple gun to staple it up on the wall. I hung the canopy with a hook we already had and then tied it by gathering it and stapling the gather. Then we stapled a tassel on the gather. We found the tassels for $.12 each on clearance after Christmas.

Elly wanted a tall princess bed, so we took identical sized boxes of books from the garage and put one under each leg. (We self-publish so we had a ton of books.) We removed the wheels from the bed frame. Then we put a board on top of the boxes for stability. Elly's bed frame is now about 15 inches feet off the ground so use the space under the bed for storing toys.

My mom made some pillows to go with Elly's comforter from material she already had. The long pink bolster was the one thing we bought retail. That was some new "extra fluffy soft" material that she purchased for about $5 for one extra special pillow.

I found a picture at the store to put on the wall behind her bed instead of a headboard. We didn't have any night stands that would work, so we stacked three boxes of books in the corner and one box in front to make a staggered "L" shaped night stand. We covered the boxes by layering a white sheet and then lace on top. She now has a nice place for her drinking cup, clock and stuffed animals.

I couldn't find curtains to match and didn't have any material to make any so I had to come up with something else. I found a white round tablecloth that I had. I ironed it, folded it in half and then draped it over her curtain rod. Then I took some fake flowers that I already had and put them on top. It turned out pretty nice for a free curtain!

We found a free standing mirror for $5 at the thrift store. There were two things wrong with it. It didn't have a base and the person had painted it black, inadvertently getting spray paint on the glass. Polish remover took off the paint in a just a couple of seconds and we simply leaned the mirror against the wall in the corner.

We made a craft table from one that the neighbors had left on the curb. It was pretty ugly, so we covered it with a tablecloth that looked nice but wouldn't be too big of a loss if she spilled something on it. Mom had a chair that was the right size, but it looked bad, too. She took some lace and tied the corners. Then she put a cluster of flowers on the back.

We also thought she needed something to hang all her art projects on. I found a corkboard that was in good shape, but had been marked up with markers, pens and crayons. I tried painting it with latex paint but the marker marks kept bleeding through. I took the blow dryer and dried the paint. I took the glue gun and hot glued some lace over the top of the cork material to cover up the marks. The paint showed through the lace but the lace covered up the marker marks.

She wanted to decorate with hearts and stars, so I took a large car washing sponge ($.75 each at Dollar General) and cut stencils out of them. I found heart and star coloring pages on the Internet and I printed them. I traced the heart and star on two sponges and then took a razor blade and cut out the edges. I only went down about 1/2 inch with the cut to remove the excess sponge. Then I put paint on the sponge and pressed it onto the wall. The sponge didn't stamp the image as well as I would have liked, so I painted over the top of the mark my stencil had made with a paintbrush.

We were able to keep Elly out of the room while I did it so she didn't really know what was going on in there. On the day of her birthday, I put a large sheet of wrapping paper over her doorframe and wrote Happy Birthday with a marker and bows. That way she could open her "present" from mom and dad. She was very excited about it!

Kids Cents

Are We Really Depriving Our Kids?

I often hear ladies complaining that they want to stay at home with their kids but that they "have to work since it is so expensive to raise kids these days". One of the main questions I get asked about frugal living is "won't I be depriving my children if I live the frugal life?" Maybe I can answer that question with a few questions.

How am I depriving my children by having them drink water for every meal instead of juice and soda? Isn't one thing doctors are always complaining about is we don't drink enough water? Cutting out just one glass of soda per person per day for a family of four would save $547.50 a year and make them healthier.

How am I depriving my children by having them eat an apple or homemade granola bar for a snack instead of a bag of chips? Obesity is a major problem among children in the United States. If you cut out just one bag of chips a week you would save $104.00 a year and make them healthier.

How am I depriving my children by having them walk to school or to a friends house instead of my always driving them there? Lack of exercise is a big problem. You would save time and wear and tear on your car by having them walk and make them healthier at the same time.

How am I depriving my children when I don't buy them every toy they see and want? We wouldn't dream of giving a baby on baby food all the chocolate that he wants because we know it would make him sick. His body can not tolerate that much chocolate even if he desires it.

In the same way, an older child can't emotionally deal with the overload of toys. I as an adult become stressed just from trying to buy a bottle of shampoo. Have you ever noticed how many options you have? Trying to make a decision can be overwhelming. Do I get it for thin, fine, dry and damaged or colored and permed hair? The list goes on and on.

In the same way when a young child looks at piles of toys, he can become very stressed over choosing which one to play with. If you watch, you will notice that they tend to play with the same couple of toys over and over. If you didn't give them all the toys they asked for and bought one less brand new toy at $10 a week, you would save $520.00 in one year and you would help relieve them of some stress.

It is no wonder our children stay confused. We insist that they should eat healthy yet we take them out to eat 3-5 times a week at McDonald's. We give them a bag of carrot sticks in their lunch because it's healthy and then give them a bag of chips when they get home from school to get them off our backs.

We want them to have strong character yet the moment they whine or cry for another toy or some candy at the store we give in out of guilt. We are afraid that if we don't give them what they want, they won't love us so to rid ourselves of uncomfortable feelings we say yes. How can we teach them to be strong in character when we are so weak?

How could our society and way of thinking have gotten so mixed up that we think a child is deprived if a mom chooses to stay home and not go to work? We have come to believe that moms should work outside the home so that children can have the most expensive clothes, education or material things. (Note I didn't say best but rather most expensive since the most expensive doesn't mean the best.) If a mom goes to work so a child can have all those things it's not considered depriving the child of anything but it's mom. Which do you think does a child more harm- being deprived expensive things or it's mom?

For you stay at home moms: Before you become too puffed up with pride be aware that too many social, church and school activities can deprive your children of you just as much as working. Do all things in moderation.

Thought for the Day

Better to give your kids your values you have
than the valuables you can't afford.

Breakfast and Snack Ideas for Picky Eaters

Many of our readers ask, **"How do I get my kids to eat?** They are so picky and I've run out of ideas..."

I think it's in a kid's nature to be picky. It's funny that kids will frown upon anything new. Our children will eat the same thing almost every day and then one day say, "I don't like sloppy Joe's". Our oldest son eats pizza but does not like sausage pizza. One day recently, he tried the sausage and loved it. He said that he loved the little meatballs. When Mike told him it was good to see him eat sausage, he suddenly wouldn't eat it. Later, we decided it was better to let him call them meatballs if that's what it took to get him to eat it! Let this be a lesson to you - If you give the kids zucchini bread, just tell them that it is "bread"! ;-)

Kids eating habits could send a family to the poor house! Between pop-tarts, fruit chews, juices boxes and containers of cool applesauce it would be easy to spend the entire month's grocery budget in one week. Here are some tips to help you find something they will eat while hanging on to some of that cash in your pocket.

Breakfast:
Are you being squeezed? - The USDA recommends two 8 oz. (1 cup) glasses of milk per day for a child. If you give your kids more than two cups a day, everything over the 2 cups is just calories, and expensive calories at that. The same is true of juice.

The USDA recommends 5 servings of fruits and vegetables a day for kids. Did you know that for children under age five, 3/4 cup of juice is one serving of fruit? How often do you fill a glass to the top with juice for your child only to find that the child doesn't drink most of it? Limit the amount of juice served to one or two small glasses a day and serve the rest of their fruit and vegetables in whole form. Whole fruits are more healthy for them than juice.

French Toast Sticks - After cooking french toast, cut each piece into 4 strips. Kids love to dip these in syrup.

126

Present oatmeal in a fancy glass such as a sundae dish. Place some granola, fruit, honey, brown sugar or nuts on top.

Stir any of the following into oatmeal:

  *sugar
  *cinnamon and sugar
  *brown sugar
  *butter or margarine
  *molasses
  *maple syrup
  *applesauce
  *chopped apples
  *dried apples
  *raisins
  *berries
  * bananas
  *chopped peaches
  *jam or jelly
  *plain or fruit yogurt
  *wheat germ
  *dark brown sugar and 1 drop of maple extract makes oatmeal taste just
      like the store bought instant oatmeal

Snack Ideas:

Have a snack sitting at the kitchen table for the kids when they come home from school. This way they won't be grouchy in the afternoon from being hungry. This will also prevent them from digging though the kitchen cabinets looking for something themselves and messing up your neat, well-organized pantry. It is also the perfect time for you to sit and visit with them about their day at school.

To discourage bad snack habits, don't buy unhealthy snacks or keep them in the house.

Present your snacks with a plate, place mat, napkin and maybe a flower from the garden. This way your snacks always look inviting.

Have jars sitting on the counter with sunflower seeds, raisins, granola, prunes or peanuts for the children. If they see healthy snacks they're more likely to want them.

Try these snacks on your kids:
  *Fresh fruit
  *Hard-boiled eggs
  *Apples, cut into quarters, with core removed
  *Popcorn balls
  *Popcorn
  *Bagels
  *Muffins
  *Dried apples or bananas
  *Breadsticks
  *Oranges, peeled and quartered
  *Pumpkin bread
  *Banana bread
  *Zucchini bread
  *Bananas
  *Crackers and cheese
  *Frozen grapes
  *Veggies with ranch dressing
  *Celery sticks, spread with peanut butter
  *Cherry tomatoes
  *Cheese

THOUGHT OF THE DAY

Be nice to your kids.
They will choose your
Nursing home one day.

Help! They're Stuffing Me!

I have discovered the secret of saving money feeding babies, toddlers and preschoolers. Well, I can't take the credit for it. My mom taught it to me many years ago but I didn't put it into practice until the first financial crisis we had when my husband was laid off.

What I have been practicing now for many years has now become one of the new buzz phrases -- "portion control". Usually when we think of portion control it is in connection with dieters and not young children or saving money.

Most American parents serve themselves and their children huge portions of food. Their families eat only part of it, and then they discard the rest. Next time you scrape those half eaten plates of food into the trash, think about this: 30% to 50% of the food and drinks we buy, whether we eat at home or out, get thrown away. That means if you are paying $500 per month on groceries, you are throwing $250 in the trash each month. If you don't believe it's true, observe your own family this week. How many half full bowls of soggy cereal do you throw away? How many pieces of toast get tossed only half eaten? What about half empty glasses of juice, milk or pop? With young children this is usually worse, but adults often do it too.

It is easy to forget that children under the age of four have only about a quarter of an adult's body weight. Often, we feed them adult portions and when we do give them smaller portions, each portion is usually only reduced to about half an adult portion. Do you use that large serving spoon and dump a full spoon of food on your child's plate? Say you give yourself two spoons of green beans and your child one-- That means that you have given yourself about 24 green beans and your child 12 when in reality, that child needs only about six.

Many parents wonder why small children resist eating everything on their plates. What if you were given double portions at every meal? When parents press kids to keep eating when they are full, they inadvertently encourage obesity. It is no wonder that we then end up throwing away half of the food left on their plates. When deciding how much food to give your kids, start small and work your way up. Remember, if they eat what is on their plates you can always give them more. If they consistently ask for seconds, then increase their portions.

Use the same method for drinks. Even a small sippy cup should only be filled half full. This not only reduces the amount that you throw away, but also reduces the losses from spills. I once heard a mom say she always bought two gallons of milk instead of just one. One gallon was for the kids to drink and the other was for them to spill.

Another great way to save a lot of money is to give children more water. In addition to serving children overly large portions, failing to give them enough water leads to obesity. At this point, many parents point out that young children need lots of milk and juice. That is true to a degree, but consider this: The USDA recommends 16 oz of milk per day for children under 4. That is equal to two sippy cups. Before you fill those two sippy cups, remember that kids get milk from other sources too, including milk with their cereal and cheese on their sandwiches. Ask any doctor and he will tell you most people are not getting enough water.

It is easy to think that if something is good for us then even more is better. That isn't always true. Fertilizer helps our lawns grow, but too much fertilizer can kill the same grass we are feeding. The same rule applies to feeding our children. We think the more juice and milk they get the better, but once kids have had as much as they need nutritionally, the rest just adds calories. Just as with adults, feeding kids too much leads to all kinds of health problems including obesity and diabetes. It also encourages them to develop bad eating habits that get more severe as they get older.

If you are ready to cut the waste from your food budget, here are a few more tips to save money and make your life easier:

1. **Cut the crust off your child's sandwich before you give it to him.** I have tried for years to get my children and grandchildren to eat the crust and have discovered that it is like trying to climb Mount Everest. It can be done, but I'm not sure if it is worth all the work and headache. So give in and cut off the crust. Throw it in a bag and use it for bread crumbs or croutons. Then the kids will eat their entire sandwiches instead of just that hole in the middle and you won't waste the sandwich filling that would have been tossed with the crust.

2. **Cut kids' sandwiches into small squares or triangles.** Their hands are smaller then ours. Imagine always manhandling sandwiches that are two to three times normal size and you can relate to kids with full adult-sized sandwiches. This goes for all their food. Cut anything they have to hold in their hands into manageable sized pieces.

3. **Spills always happen, but they can be minimized.** Try placing a paper doily at the top of your child's plate or someplace where you know a cup won't be likely to spill. Then teach the child that the cup belongs on the doily. Even the youngest child will learn quickly to always place his cup back on the doily and out of harm's way.

4. **Start giving your little ones only half of items like candy bars,** gum, and popsicles. When you go out to eat, split a hamburger or order of fries between two younger children. You can even ask for an extra cup and split milk shakes and drinks. Better yet, just order water. Save the milkshakes and drinks for a special treat and the kids will appreciate them more.

5. **Control snacks.** Don't just let the kids graze all day on candy and chips. Give children healthier things to fill them up, like popcorn or a piece of fruit at specific time intervals.

6. **Feed toddlers and preschoolers your leftovers.** They usually don't balk at them like older children do. All those two tablespoon leftovers that are hardly worth saving are usually just the right amount for younger children.

THOUGHT OF THE DAY

If you have a lot of tension
And you get a headache,
Do what it says
On the aspirin bottle:

"Take two aspirin
and Keep Away From Children!!!!"

The Great Milk Crisis

I rushed to my computer to write this when I heard the news. I knew there would be a great panic over it and thought I could hopefully calm some fears. What was the news? Was it something earth shattering like flood, epidemic, or war? No! But it made the headlines - "The price of milk is going up!" I could hear the panic in the newscaster's voice and the trembling in "Mrs. Woman-on-the-street's" voice as she answered his question, "What will you do now?"

"I guess I will have to just start watering down my children's milk because they just love it so much." Then she took a deep heart wrenching sigh... Of course, I'm telling you this with tongue in cheek. We live in a world of panic and fear. I try to put these things in perspective. I mean compared to the Great Depression, the Dust Bowl (for those of you who aren't up on your history, that's not a new football game ;-), the flu epidemic of 1917, and World Wars I and II, the fact that the price of milk is going up 50 cents ranks pretty low on my list of things to panic about.

No, I don't have lots of money to throw away. At this time in my life I am pretty much living off the same amount or less than most people on welfare or some elderly people on social security so any price increase is hard on me too.

What I found most interesting was the next item of news after the earth shattering milk scare. It was about a new "apple" that is coming out on Friday and everyone can hardly wait to buy one for $500. I mean to me, paying $2.50 for three pounds of apples is outrageous, let alone spending $500 for one apple! OK, I've got my tongue in my cheek once again! Even though my children think I am completely computer illiterate, I do realize that the new "Apple" they were talking about was some sort of fancy hand held computer/telephone/phone (I think ;-).

Here's my point: We sometimes have our priorities goofy. These people were horrified at having to pay an extra 50 cents for milk -- food that they really needed for their children, but they thought nothing of having to pay $500 for what basically amounts to a new electrical toy.

Having milk prices go up is irritating yes, but it is not the end of the world. (Having my Hershey's candy bar double in price over night -- now that is something to panic over. HA! HA! Talk about priorities! ;-) Before you come unglued each time you hear that the price of bread, milk or gas is raised, try putting it into perspective.

I don't want you to think I am taking this whole thing too lightly. I do want to help make things a little easier for you, so here are some tips to help you save if the price of milk is getting out of control in your area. Most of these basic principles can be used with any food item whose price is getting higher than you would like.

One of the main ways to save on milk is portion control. You have heard me say again and again that we need to start seriously controlling the amount and portion size of the food we give our children. The woman in the news interview above said she would just have to dilute the milk for her children. That really isn't the best solution and usually all that does is to make the milk taste nasty. Now that I think about it, I guess that would be one way to keep the kids from drinking more of it but it's not really the best idea.

A better solution is to have the children drink water more often. Use milk (and juice) only as part of the nutritional value of the meal, not as a primary way to quench thirst. When you plan your menu, if you have cheese or yogurt for your meal, you don't have to serve milk because you already have your dairy. Let everyone drink water. If there is no dairy in the meal, give them a proper serving of milk (6-8 oz. not 16 oz. which is the size of a lot of glasses used at meals).

Waste not want not. This good old fashioned saying really is true. Stop wasting milk. How much milk is left in that half eaten bowl of cereal and poured down the drain each morning? What about that large glass of milk that you poured for your child who drank only half of it? The average American family could cut the amount of milk they buy by 50% just by controlling portion sizes and waste. (That includes that sour milk in the fridge that always gets thrown out).

Stop your children from using the "dump" method with their cereal. You know what I mean, they pour out the cereal, not paying attention to what they are doing, until there is a huge mound in their bowl. Then they pour in enough milk to equal the portion of cereal they have dumped in. You may have to take the time and effort to pour the kids' milk in their cereal bowls for a while to help cut back until they learn to use the right amount themselves. Sometimes something as simple as pouring the milk into a pitcher that is smaller and easier for a child to handle can help. I find a gallon of milk hard to pour so I can't imagine how a young child can handle it properly. I use a small pitcher for my kids and grandkids and they have always loved getting to use the cute little pitcher. I think it is one of those "little things" that helps make their lives easier and they appreciate that.

Make foods that don't use as much milk. Instead of having cereal every morning, make oatmeal, eggs and toast, or pancakes. I like to use milk even if my pancake mix calls for water but you can change that to half milk and half water and it will still taste good. Instead of making pudding for dessert, make a pan of brownies or cupcakes from a box that calls for no milk. Having company this summer? Think watermelon instead of homemade ice cream.

Watch for milk that is marked down and buy all that you can. Most people don't realize that you can freeze milk. All you have to do is be sure you shake it well after you thaw it. Find out when your store stocks the milk or mark it down. I was at a store just yesterday and there was a man putting some cheese on the shelves. I simply asked him when they stocked their dairy products and what time. He didn't mind telling me at all.

As much as I hate to admit how old I am, I have lived many years now and one thing I have found is the price of food always changes - up and down, this way and that - but it is nothing to panic over. Everything usually balances out in the end. Just adjust your eating habits accordingly and you will do fine. Besides, over time most incomes usually end up adjusting to the price of things, so it all balances out.

Hopefully, you can now enjoy your next glass of milk... but watch out for those terribly expensive "apples"!

Chill Out This Summer

The day moms dread all year long has arrived: the last day of school and the first day of summer vacation. Try these recipes to help the kids chill out:

Snow Cones
Crushed Ice
1 pkg. flavored drink mix (flavor of your choice)

Mix drink mix with half as much water as the directions indicate. Chill 1 hour. Just before serving, crush some ice. You can use either a snow cone maker or put some ice cubes in a plastic bag and pound with hammer. Pack ice chips into cups, pour chilled drink mix over the ice and serve. You can also use fruit juice boiled down to half with food coloring added.
Apple juice: green or red food coloring
Grape juice: purple food coloring

Frozen Bananas
bananas
skewers (optional)

Cut bananas in half crosswise. Insert skewer in the thicker end. Place bananas on a tray and place in freezer. When frozen, move to a plastic bag and keep frozen until ready to use.

Toppings
yogurt
nuts, finely chopped
peanut butter applesauce
melted chocolate coconut
wheat germ

Allow bananas to thaw slightly. Put toppings in small bowls. Dip banana before each bite. Eat plain or roll or dip into any of the toppings. Use the wet topping first so the others will stick.

Play Dough

2 cups flour
1 cup salt
1 tsp. cream of tartar

2 Tbsp. oil
2 cups water
food coloring

Mix together all ingredients except food coloring in a saucepan. Cook over medium heat, stirring constantly until mixture gathers on the spoon and forms dough (about 6 minutes). Dump onto waxed paper until cool enough to handle and knead until pliable. Store in a covered container or plastic bag. Add food coloring for different colors. Makes about 2 pounds.

Easy Finger Paints

1/4 cup cornstarch
2 cups water

Mix in saucepan and boil until thick. Then pour into a jar and add food coloring until the desired shade is achieved. Store covered in the refrigerator.

Finger Paints

1 pkg. unflavored gelatin
1/2 cup cold water
1/2 cup cornstarch

1 1/2 cups water
liquid dish detergent
food coloring

Dissolve gelatin in 1/2 cup water. Set aside. In a saucepan add cornstarch then slowly stir in 1 1/2 cups water until well blended over medium heat. Cook until it boils, becomes smooth, thickens and turns clear. Add gelatin mixture and stir well. Pour into containers and add a drop of liquid dish detergent. Add food coloring until you get the desired shade. Store covered in the refrigerator 4 - 6 weeks.

Popsicle Paradise!

Remember when you used to sit on your front steps on a hot summer day eating a popsicle? It was usually red or purple and on special occasions you got a fudgesicle. Remember how you tried to lick the drips faster than the sun could melt them? Sometimes the drips would roll down your fingers, forcing you to make the mind numbing decision whether to lick your fingers or the new drips forming on your popsicle.

Every once in a while a few drips would get out of control and fall on your bare toes. Remember how your dog's tongue felt like sandpaper when he licked the sweet gooeyness off of them?
Making your own popsicles can give great variety and keep your kids cool this summer!

It's funny how we try to make drama and expensive memories for our children when it's the simple everyday things we remember the most.

Try some of these ideas to keep the kids entertained this summer:

To find popsicle molds, look at discount and mail order stores or garage sales. If you don't have any molds, use small paper or plastic cups. Put a wooden stick or plastic spoon in the center.

For mini popsicles, pour orange, apple or grape juice or flavored drink mix into ice cube trays. Partially freeze and then place toothpicks in the center of each cube (or place plastic wrap over the top, secure and insert toothpicks through plastic wrap).

For non-traditional popsicles:

* **Freeze applesauce in popsicle molds.**

* **Mix fruit or jam into yogurt.** Freeze in small, snack sized Ziploc bags for frozen yogurt on the go. Cut a hole in the end of the bag for easy access/eating.

* **Mix gelatin and freeze.** Add gummie fish or worms before freezing for added fun.

* Freeze syrup from canned fruit.

* Add food coloring or sprinkles to yogurt or softened ice cream for added pizzazz. Then freeze in popsicle molds.

* When you have leftover jam or jelly, put 1/4 cup of hot water in the jar and shake well. Pour into popsicle molds and freeze.

* If jelly or jam doesn't set up well, use for popsicles or add more water, boil and make syrup.

* Make a batch of pudding. Add coconut, nuts, marshmallows, crushed cookies or sprinkles if desired. Pour into molds. Freeze several hours until firm.

* Stick a toothpick in the center of blackberries, strawberries, raspberries or sliced bananas. Dip in chocolate if desired. Freeze on a tray. Once frozen, store in freezer bags.

* For easy snow cones, freeze orange juice (or any other flavored juice) in ice cube trays. Store frozen juice cubes in a plastic bag. Blend 5 cubes in the blender until they have a shaved ice consistency. The shaved ice will keep its consistency if kept frozen in a container.

* For watermelon popsicles, blend one cup each watermelon chunks (seeds removed), orange juice and water. Blend well. Then pour and freeze into molds.

* For strawberry popsicles, blend 2 cups strawberries, 1 cup vanilla ice cream or yogurt, 4 cups orange juice and 2 tablespoons sugar. Blend smooth. Pour into molds and freeze.

* For banana popsicles, dissolve one 3 oz. package strawberry gelatin with one cup boiling water. In a blender, mix gelatin, 1 banana and 1 cup yogurt or ice cream. Blend well and pour into molds.

Pudding Pops

1 pkg. pudding (not instant*)
3 cups milk

Combine 1 large package of pudding with 3 cups of milk. Mix only enough to blend well. Quickly pour into popsicle molds and freeze. Chocolate and vanilla pudding may be layered for a fun treat. Makes 8-10 popsicles.
*Regular homemade pudding may be used instead of store-bought pudding mix.

BEFORE AND AFTER CHILDREN

BEFORE CHILDREN: I was thankful for holistic medicine and natural herbs.
AFTER CHILDREN: I am thankful for pediatric cough syrup guaranteed to "cause drowsiness" in young children.

BEFORE CHILDREN: I was thankful for the opportunity to vacation in exotic foreign countries so I could experience a different way of life in a new culture.
AFTER CHILDREN: I am thankful to have time to make it all the way down the driveway to get the mail.

BEFORE CHILDREN: I was thankful for the Moosewood Vegetarian cookbook.
AFTER CHILDREN: I am thankful for the butterball turkey hotline.

BEFORE CHILDREN: I was thankful for a warm, cozy home to share with my loved ones.
AFTER CHILDREN: I am thankful for the lock on the bathroom door.

BEFORE CHILDREN: I was thankful for material objects like custom furniture, a nice car and trendy clothes.
AFTER CHILDREN: I am thankful when the baby spits up and misses my good shoes.

When Does School Start?

The kids have been out of school for weeks now. You're lying in your hammock with a gentle summer breeze softly cooling you and the sweet smell of summer flowers fills the air. Yeah, Right! Reality check! You have probably heard "I'm bored. I have nothing to do" a hundred times today!

Don't run down the street panicking, wildly flinging your arms and screaming like a mad woman. I say this not because of what the neighbors might think. Most of the other moms would probably be hard on your heels. I just don't believe in using any more energy than necessary.

Instead, peel Tarzan off the chandelier and catch Superman in the midst of his fifth flight from the top bunk bed, trying carefully not to tear his cape made from your favorite red silk blouse. With your free hand grab child #3 who is painting a great copy of the Mona Lisa on your bedroom wall.

March the kids to the kitchen (there may be some resistance but you will prevail) and try these recipes. Who knows? Between these and a small miracle you might just get to swing in the hammock yet. (But then again, probably not!)

Edible Play Dough

1/3 cup margarine
1/3 cup light corn syrup
1/2 tsp. salt
1 tsp. vanilla extract or flavorings
1 lb. powdered sugar
food coloring (optional)

Mix first 4 ingredients together. Add powdered sugar. Knead it. Divide and add food coloring. Keep refrigerated to keep from spoiling when not in use. You can replace vanilla with flavored extracts to give flavor other than just plain sweetness.

Slime
1/2 cup white glue
6 Tbsp. water
food coloring
1-4 tsp. Borax
1-4 Tbsp. water

Mix the glue, 6 tablespoons water and food coloring until it is dissolved. In a separate bowl, dissolve 1 teaspoon borax into 1 tablespoon water. Add to the glue solution. You will get a very thick clump of slime when the two mix. Pull the clump of slime out of the glue mixture and put it in a separate bowl. Mix another batch of the borax solution and add to the remaining glue mixture. Repeat until all the glue mixture is used (about 3-4 times). With clean hands, knead the slime to mix. This will take about 10 minutes and is not very difficult as the slime easily separates between your fingers. If a looser, more slimy texture, is desired knead in a bit more water. The more water you add, the slimier it gets. The slime doesn't leave a residue and doesn't get stuck on anything. This is great for Halloween entertaining. Store in an airtight container. This can easily be doubled, tripled or quadrupled.

Homemade Bubbles

1/4 cup liquid dishwashing detergent*
1/2 cup water
1 Tbsp. sugar

Put the dishwashing detergent in the water. Carefully stir in sugar trying to avoid suds. Take a regular drinking straw and cut into 4 pieces. Then dip into the solution and blow your bubbles. Tie a rope loop up to a foot in diameter on the end of a stick and make a gallon of bubbles. Dip the rope in the bubbles and run with them. This will give you giant bubbles.
* Dawn non-ultra dish detergent works best. You can find it in small stores such as Dollar General.

Save $400 on school lunches this year!

These days in America, it seems that everyone is so busy that preparing school lunches is liable to push a typical mom right over the edge. When you have to choose between making school lunches or spending that extra 15 minutes in bed, it seems like buying ready made lunches at the store is a no-brainer, but your budget doesn't agree.

The average mom packs $2.00 worth of pre-packaged goodies into each lunch she sends to school with her kids. (That works out to $720 for 2 kids.) What mother hasn't wondered if those lunches are even getting eaten?

Try these tips for things you can do in 30 minutes or less on the weekend to make those school lunches a snap!

* **Those snack bags of munchies cost a lot!** Make your own by pre-packaging chips, pretzels, animal crackers and other snack items into sandwich bags on the weekends. (Have the kids help!) Store them in a big container or basket and just throw them in the lunch box in the morning.

* **Let the kids create their own Pizza lunch kits-** Toast bread and cutout little circles with a biscuit cutter. Add small containers of pizza sauce, cheese, and other toppings.

* **Make fruit gelatin and pudding** and put in small plastic containers for the week. Make a large batch of granola bars, cookies, pumpkin bread, banana bread or muffins. Divide them into zip top sandwich bags and freeze so that you can grab one or two when needed.

* **Brownie bites are simple to make.** Bake brownie mix in mini-muffin pans and put three "brownie bites" in a sandwich bag for each child's lunch. They freeze well too!

* **Fill thermos (not glass) half full with juice** the night before and it will be cold when the kids are ready to drink it and it keeps their food cold.

* **Clean vegetables, slice into pieces and bag.** Preparing a weeks worth of veggies at a time for lunches and snacks saves money and time.

* **Purchase cheese in blocks,** cut into pieces and put in sandwich bags.

* **Save napkins, catsup and mustard packets** you get from take-out. Use in lunches.

THOUGHT OF THE DAY

Children seldom misquote you.
In fact, they usually repeat word for word
What you shouldn't have said.

*****

Grandchildren are God's reward
For not killing your own children.

Make Your Own Custom Lunch Box

Have you ever looked for a lunch box that your child would like only to settle for something that you knew wouldn't quite do the job? I have more than once found myself frustrated because all the lunch boxes I could find were either too expensive, too cheaply made or featured characters my kids didn't like on the front. One year, after keeping my eye out for a lunch box for BJ for some time, I ended up buying a plain soft sided lunch box from Wal-Mart. I wasn't too excited about the quality of the lunch box, (It was one of those cheap soft sided vinyl ones.) but since I had to settle for one that wasn't what I wanted, I bought one of the less expensive ones.

After a few months use, the lunch box just shredded. I wasn't surprised, but I was back to square one.

BJ still used the rapidly deteriorating lunch box for a few weeks while I looked for a replacement, but in that time I couldn't find anything. Finally, it kicked the bucket and I needed to find something that weekend.

We had an old Pokeman lunchbox that was just a spare. I think we bought it at a garage sale for a quarter. It was one of the hard plastic ones that is usually a little more durable. No one really likes Poke man in our family, but we went ahead and got that lunch box to keep as a cheap emergency replacement.

Even though he never liked Pokemon, BJ does have one great love in life. He is just wild over Furbies. The kid is Furby crazy!! If you don't remember Furbies, they were one of those toys that people would stand in long lines overnight to buy for their kids back in the early 90's. Of course, it's great when your child loves a craze after the mania is all over because you can find the things to collect at garage sales and thrift stores for cheap! Most of BJ's Furbies cost a quarter or less.

I decided since I couldn't find a good quality lunch box he would like, I would make him a Furby lunch box.

I found some Furby clip art on the Internet and printed some of the ones I thought he would like. (I didn't think of it at the time, but I could have taken pictures of his Furbies with a digital camera and printed them instead.) Then I cut them out and glued them on a piece of white paper that I had already cut to the size of the lunch box face to make sure the entire Poke man logo was covered.

Once I had the Furbies glued to the paper the way I wanted it, I glued the paper with Elmer's glue to the lunchbox. Then I covered it with contact paper. I trimmed the contact paper to size with a razor blade and put a bead of glue around the edge to "seal" it.

After letting it sit all night, it hadn't dried, so I set it in the sun to dry that day. Unfortunately, the glue never dried and then the clip art faded. Sometimes it takes more than one try to get it right.

I started all over again and this time I did everything the same except I used glue made specifically for plastic. It worked perfectly!

The lunch box was a huge hit with BJ and right away, Elly wanted her own "special" lunch box. I made a lunch box for her the same way, using My Little Pony art. It only cost me a few minutes worth of work, even considering that I had to re-do it the first time. This "custom lunchbox" has worked well for BJ for more than a year. At some point, he will want a different lunch box and since the hard plastic lunch box is still holding up well, I will probably reuse the same one with new art the next time.

Strength is the capacity to break a chocolate bar into four pieces with your bare hands – and then eat just one of the pieces. - Judith Viorst

Back To School, Or Back To The Poor House?

I walked into Wal-Mart today and saw her standing there: a mom. She had two children sitting in her shopping cart, one walking beside it and another clinging to her leg. She had the look of a battle weary soldier, with her feet dragging and her shoulders slumped. Child #1 was punching child #3. Child #2 was begging for a toy and child #4 was doing the "potty dance".

As she approached the main aisle of the store she looked up and saw the display there. Her face lit up. She smiled and straightened her shoulders. There was joy and hope shining from her like I had never seen before.

You may ask "What was on that display that caused this mom to break forth in song singing, "Oh, What a Beautiful Morning?" Was it spectacular jewelry or the latest in designer dresses? Oh, no no no! It was school supplies! For decades, moms everywhere have eagerly awaited the day when that first box of crayons and pack of notebook paper make their appearance.

For many, though, the first reaction of joy is quickly followed by a second reaction of pure dread. "How am I going to pay for all of this?" I sat last year and watched as a TV news reporter asked person after person at one store how much they had just spent for school supplies. I was shocked at the amounts people were spending. I couldn't figure out what was going on. How could it cost $1000 for school supplies? Yes, you heard it right -- $1000.

Basic supplies like crayons, pencils and notebook paper cost only about half the price of what they cost 20 years ago. In our school district, the basic items only costs around $15 and that includes an inexpensive backpack.

So what was the problem with the people on the news? Suddenly I noticed something interesting. Each person's shopping cart wasn't full of school supplies, it was full of clothes, shoes, and the latest in aerodynamic backpacks, some of which cost nearly as much as the first car my husband and I bought.

If you find that back to school preparation throws your finances out of balance, try these tips to help bring back to school costs back within your budget:

Make sure what you are buying is only what your children absolutely need and not simply what they want to make them "cool". Expensive clothes, shoes, purses and lunch pails are not needs but wants. You don't need to buy the best and most expensive backpacks in the world. One woman said that she paid $100 for her child's backpack because she felt it would last longer. She was sure she got the better deal. She was proud that it lasted 3 years. Financially speaking, she could have bought two less expensive backpacks each year for three years and it still would have been cheaper than the one $100 backpack. More expensive isn't always better.

If the school's required supply list calls for a 24 count box of crayons, don't buy a 96 count box. One teacher begged her parents to send only the 24 count box because the 24 box gives children some choice without overwhelming them. A five to eight year old can spend ages agonizing over what color to color something and too much choice slows things down in class.

Don't buy everything at once. I have yet to understand how it could be that, the week before school starts, every child in the United States no longer has a stitch of clothing to wear and needs to have a whole new wardrobe. I think it is one of those traditions that we have followed for decades just because, as far as we can remember, it has always been done that way.

You have probably heard the story of the woman who always cut the ends off her ham before she baked it. When asked why she did that she said because her mom did it that way. When the mom was asked why she did it that way she said because her mom had done it that way, too. When grandma was asked the same question, she said "because I didn't have a big enough pan and I had to cut it to make it fit".

Years ago, most kids only had one or two outfits and those were generally work clothes. When they started school, they often got new school clothes because their clothes were actually worn out. They needed something a little better and something that wasn't too small. Since they had gone barefoot all summer and winter was coming, many would get a new pair of shoes. So started a tradition. Most children now have reasonable clothes that they have been wearing all summer and can probably wear to school. If your children really need new jeans, get them one or two pairs now and then, in a month or so, buy them another pair.

So often we have an all or nothing mentality. I need gas, so instead of just putting in the $15 cash that I have in my pocket right now that would last a couple of days, I think I need to fill the tank and put it on my almost overloaded credit card. (Then later when I get the urge to buy a soda at a convenience store, I'll rationalize "I've got the cash in my pocket, so I can afford it.")

You don't need to buy your children a year's worth of clothes the week before school. I know there are a lot of good buys just before school, but if you have to charge them on a high interest credit card, they are no longer good buys.

Try to make do with what you already have. If the kids still have scissors from last year, reuse them. That goes for rulers, pencil boxes and other supplies, too. Go ahead and buy new crayons (they cost 20 cents a box here in back to school sales), folders and pencils. That way your children feel like they are getting something new.

If last year's backpack is still good then reuse it. If your child wants something different, then use glue or fusible web and appliqué it with some fun trims and decorations. If they still insist that they need a new backpack, let them take their own money and buy one.

From A Reader

Thank you for your newsletter about back to school & buying school clothes. I had already purchased perfectly good clothes for my daughter this summer at garage sales, but like many others, was planning on buying "school clothes". Why? I don't know, because it's just been one of those things people do without even considering why.

When I read that newsletter, it was like a lightning bolt - of course, if the clothes she's been wearing are in good condition, why go & buy more just because school is starting? You saved us a good deal of money, I'm sure, as well as many others who read that newsletter. It's all about changing the way we think about things - that's the real key to saving money. Thanks again!

-Chantelle H.

BEFORE AND AFTER CHILDREN

BEFORE CHILDREN: I was thankful to have been born the USA, the post powerful free democracy in the world.
AFTER CHILDREN: I am thankful for Velcro tennis shoes. As well as saving valuable time, now I can hear the sound of my son taking off his shoes -- which gives me three extra seconds to activate the safety locks on the back seat windows right before he hurls them out of the car and onto the freeway.

BEFORE CHILDREN: I was thankful for the recycling program which will preserve our natural resources and prevent the overloading of landfills.
AFTER CHILDREN: I am thankful for swim diapers because every time my son wanders into water in plain disposables, he ends up wearing a blimp the size of, say, New Jersey, on his bottom.

BEFORE CHILDREN: I was thankful for fresh, organic vegetables.
AFTER CHILDREN: I am thankful for microwaveable macaroni and cheese -- without which my children would be surviving on about three bites of cereal and their own spit.

BEFORE CHILDREN: I was thankful for the opportunity to obtain a college education and have a higher quality of life than my ancestors.
AFTER CHILDREN: I am thankful to finish a complete thought without being interrupted.

Kids' Birthday Parties

Corlin writes: **I have a daughter who is turning 5 this month and I usually spend too much on the whole thing.** Do you have any suggestions on how to cut the cost? We are having it at home this year. I plan to make cheese and crackers and veggie and fruit platters. Any other short cuts?

Tawra: **We keep our parties simple.** We usually only provide cake and ice cream for food and Kool-aid for drinks. We also limit the number of kids to between 5-7 friends if a lot of family will be there so we don't have more than 15 people with family. We didn't have parties with friends from school until our son turned eight and our daughter turned seven. Prior to that, we only had family parties.

It is helpful if there are several adults present to make sure everything goes smoothly. We usually have one adult working on cake, another re-filling punch and possibly another just making sure the kids are doing well.

Here are some details of our first two parties with their school friends:

BJ's Party

This was the first party I've thrown for one of the kids. It ended up being really nice and I learned some things too!

First, we sent out invitations but no one called. I had to call everyone and they all said they were coming. I'm glad I called because I would have expected no one to show up!

One kid brought his sibling (The mom didn't tell me she planned to bring him). I now know to buy extra party favors. Mike asked me if I had prepared for a few extra kids and I said no because I didn't think everyone would show up. Sometimes you have to improvise. We ended up telling our kids and my niece and nephew that we would give them something else later.

For party favors I bought some bags of fall Hershey's kisses on clearance for $1.30 each. We had a treasure hunt and the bags of kisses were sitting in a basket at the end of the treasure hunt trail. (If you live in a hot climate like we do, this is not the time of the year for chocolate waiting for kids to find it outside!)

About the treasure hunt: We made ten clues that sent them running all over the place. We have a half acre yard and we sent them from the back of the lot over to the neighbor's house two houses away, about a half block back and forth. That was way too much. We made 10 clues and they were completely worn out from running so much. Some had to sit down and rest before they were done. Next time I will make 10 clues, but have them clustered closer together so that they follow clues between the front and back yard only. Even though they were tired, they still loved it!

We made a pin the tail on the Furby game and played "Furby Says" ("Simon Says" with a Furby theme ;-). I drew a Furby and painted it on brown paper that I had. Then we cut out tails out of white paper and put the kid's names on them. They enjoyed it too.

It's funny, because even though the kids liked the games, they would have much rather just played on our swing set (which cost us $20) and our tire swing (free). The kids were actually more excited about playing together in the yard than they were about playing structured games.

The kids had just as much fun at our homespun party as they had at other parties where parents rented gymnastics clubs, paid for swimming at the YMCA or took the kids to some other costly venue. I was excited that I didn't have to spend a lot of money for the kids to have a good time. Since I hadn't ever done this before, I was wondering if some would complain that it was "boring" just playing in our backyard, but they still remember that party fondly today.

For decorations, I used crape paper that I found at a garage sale for .25. I bought balloons, napkins, plates and cups for $1 each at a dollar store.

We covered the table with brown paper (we've had a huge roll of it for years) and lined the Furbies down the middle.

I made the Furby Cake myself by making a 9x13 cake and putting one of BJ's Furby toys in the middle. Then I just piped on a purple border using a decorating bag and that was it! The cake cost $1.25.

I was able to do the entire party for:

$14.30 party favors
$4.25 for decorations and invitations
$1.25 for the cake
.40 for Kool-aid
Total = $20.20

I was trying to keep it under $25 so I was excited that it cost even less than that!

Everyone had a blast and it was easy clean up. It was 70° outside so we were able to have the party on the deck (God was showing favor on me! :-) so I didn't even have to vacuum!

Elly's Party

We decided to have a big party for Elly and 13 kids from school came over. It worked out great.

First God was good and it was 55° outside (Her birthday is in January and we live in Kansas.) so they could go out and play on the swing set and tire swing while everyone was coming. We were also able to play our games outside. (No, 55 degrees isn't even close to being normal for January in Kansas!)

Elly wanted a penguin party. For decorations, I put a dark blue piece of material I had on the table. I used regular white paper plates and napkins and then purchased some white disposable cups for $2. We put her white Christmas tree with penguin ornaments for the centerpiece and her set her stuffed penguins out around it.

We decorated the room with streamers. We purchased them from a garage sale for .25. Mom found a 36" hanging penguin on clearance for .50 after Christmas and we hung that down from the center of the ceiling fan with some balloons ($2).

For games, we planned a race where the kids carried baby stuffed animals between their legs, like penguins do, across the yard to see who would get to the finish line first. We also did a treasure hunt. The treasure was a bag of assorted candy for each child that we bagged using after Christmas clearance candy. (About $2) We set them all over the front yard for the end of the treasure hunt. (Yes, we learned not to send them to the next state for the treasure hunt this time! ;-)

I made the penguin cake, which took a long time, but it did turn out cute. I burned the first cake so the total cost was about $2 for the cakes. :-)

I had a Victorian dollhouse that I started putting together when I was 18 years old. I never did get it all done. Well, Elly has wanted that thing for years, so I spent two weeks during David's naps fixing it up. It really needed a lot of work, but it turned out cute and she loved it!

The party turned out really nice.

I think all together we spent about $20 for everything for her party and gifts.

As you can probably see, if you put a little imagination into your parties, you can give your kids great parties without a lot of cost. Generally, kids will appreciate these parties just as much as expensive hosted parties.

THOUGHT OF THE DAY

The main purpose of holding children's parties
is to remind yourself that there are children
more awful than your own.

153

Examples of Clues for Kids Party Treasure Hunts

Often when we have a party for the kids, we make a treasure hunt for them. if you decide to have a treasure hunt, here is an example of some of the clues we have used in the past. Keep in mind you don't have to be a brilliant poet to be successful. The kids are more excited about where they are going next than about the literary value of the poetry!

If you have never had a treasure hunt for your kids, make it so that the kids are a little bit challenged to find the clues but not too challenged. We usually give them a location of the next clue, but the clue is generally somewhat hidden at that location. We have also learned that it is not a good idea to spread out the clues over a large geographic area. We once had a treasure hunt where the kids had to go to a neighbor's house a half a block away for some of the clues. Even though young children have a lot of energy, they quickly lose interest if it is too difficult to reach the goal.

The last tip is to make sure you put the location of the clue in the last sentence. I didn't do that and the kids start running before they finish reading if the location isn't in the last line.

Sample Treasure Hunt Clues
No, they don't all rhyme. I was going brain dead by the time I did them. ;-)

1. Happy Birthday Dear Elly!
   It's Time to Look For The Clues
   Everyone Jump Up and Yell WAHOO!!!
   Look Under the Stairs for Clue #2!!

2. Jump for Glee
   When You Find Clue #3
   Under the Birdbath,
   It Will Be!!

3. Are You Ready To Go,
   Out by the Garage Door,
   Sitting On The Chair is Clue #4

4. For #5 To The Back of the Yard We Go,
   Under the bucket, Oh No!
   Don't worry -- it's not a mile!
   Hurry to the Compost Pile.

5. Don' t Worry About Finding It,
   It Really Won't Be Hard!
   Clue #6 Is under the fireplace in the fort.

6. Don't Bonk Your Head!
   Clue #7 is Under The Deck.
   Be Careful When You Look, it's hanging on the wall.

7. The treasure, Where is it Found?!
   Run Quick, but not too hard
   Out to the Front Yard!

For this party, all of the clues were in our back yard and the treasure was in the front yard. We made bags of assorted candy for each child so that everyone who attended the party received a gift bag at the end of the treasure hunt. Adapt this concept to your own party and they will have lots of fun!

Teens Don't Have to Cost
More Than Babies!

Whenever my daughter Tawra talks about how to live frugally, she can always count on one type of feedback -- from people who say, "You don't understand what it's like. You have young children and not teenagers. Teenagers cost more!" Most of the advice and tips that Tawra shares come from me. I have raised two teenagers on a very minimal income. My main goal in raising my children was to teach them to become responsible and productive adults. By the time they hit their teen years, they were contributing to the household income, not depleting it.

I have never understood why people always say "wait until you have teenagers". I waited and the huge cost that I had heard about never materialized.

My house payment was the same when I had babies as it was when I had teenagers. If the house payment changes, it's not because of the age of the children but because we want a house that we think is better than the one we already have.

My utilities didn't increase because I had teenagers. If anything they went down, because instead of having to fill a big tub full of water to give my little ones a bath, I taught my teens to take a quick shower, which used less water. I didn't do as much laundry because I no longer had to wash diapers. Even when I used disposables, I still had to change my babies and toddlers clothes several times a day because they spit up on them, spilled things on them or had potty training accidents. If you have had a teenage boy, you know that until he got his first girlfriend, he would have worn the same clothes day and night if you'd let him!

I admit that I spent a little more on food, but even in that case it wasn't so much more that it led me to financial ruin the way some people make it seem. When my granddaughter was born, my daughter spent more for her special formula then I spent on food for my teenage son!

As far as clothes go, I didn't find teenagers much more expensive than young children. The cost for disposable diapers really adds up and since babies and young children grow quickly, you have to buy them an entire new wardrobe every 3-6 months. Once teenagers reach high school, they have pretty much stopped growing so quickly and many teenagers don't wear their clothes out as quickly as young children.

I can hear someone protesting, "…but teens need to have special clothes so they can be like their peers!" I could write a whole book on this point alone, but let me just give you a few hints and ideas. First, you don't have to spend a lot to dress nicely. There are garage sales, second hand stores and hand me downs. If you aren't a snob about wearing second hand clothes, your kids won't be either.

Make your teens feel loved and secure at home. You'll find that even though the way they dress and look is still important, it won't become the be-all and end-all of everything! Not only that, if they feel loved at home, it will go a long way toward keeping them out of the trouble so many parents dread.

I provided my children with the basics in their wardrobe. A pair of tennis shoes, dress shoes, three or four pairs of jeans, two pairs of dress pants, pajamas and some shirts. For anything else they wanted to have, or if they wanted to "upgrade", they paid for those items themselves. They had to work for the extras by babysitting, doing yard work and finding other ways to get a little spending money. By age fifteen, my daughter was working part time at a hospital flower shop two evenings a week.

People often fear that working will negatively affect their kids' grades. It won't. Teenagers have more time and energy then they know what to do with. Why do you think drugs, drinking and the lazy party attitude is so rampant among teens? I'm not saying that they should work 40 hours a week, but a part-time job doesn't hurt anything and it teaches responsibility! Generations past understood this, and expected their teens to work. They knew that it would prepare them for responsible adulthood. Recent generations haven't taught this, which is why so many adult children mooch off of their parents.

When a child is born, we give him everything he needs or wants every time he cries. When he's a toddler, we wouldn't dream of giving him chocolate for every meal, even though he cries for it. Yet when teenagers whine and complain for something that they want, many people just buy it for them, instead of letting them work for it.

What an injustice we do our children when we give up the opportunity to teach them because we are tired of hearing their complaints and challenges. Instead of using their last years living with us to teach them to be responsible, productive, hard workers, we often teach them to be dependent. I know a good education can help a person get a good job, but that education is of no use in a job if the person isn't a responsible, productive, hard worker with some kind of experience.

In the same way we teach a baby to go from milk to soft food to solid food we need to help our children to build up their "life's muscles" concerning finances gradually. By the time the kids are teenagers, that will require some "heavy lifting" on your part. How wrong parents are to give their children everything they ask for. If you do, you will be wondering why your grown child won't move out, why he can't hold down a job and why he is such a poor money manager.

Incidentally, my teenagers graduated with A's, my daughter received a scholarship to a university in Sweden and my son went to school to learn drafting. They are now very responsible, independent, productive adults and parents. Teenagers don't have to cost more than small children if you are wise in the way you raise and teach them.

THOUGHT OF THE DAY

Mothers of teens now know why
Some animals eat their young.

Cloth Diapering Hints

If you are considering cloth diapers, here is my story. Among other things, I will explain how I wash my cloth diapers and how many you need to start. Many people have many different motives for using cloth diapers, but my motivation is purely to save money. I do use disposable diapers for traveling because it is more difficult to store dirty diapers when I'm not at home.

I love my cloth diapers! I LOVE THEM!!!! My husband doesn't even mind using them. We found that they are not really any more difficult to use than disposables, except that we have to do more laundry. We also found that our children had much less trouble with diaper rash when in cloth rather than disposable. For a while, I had two children in cloth but now my son is potty trained. My daughter is starting to potty train so soon I won't have any in diapers.

You don't need many to start. You can start with one dozen and just wash everyday. Two dozen does make life easier. I buy the good quality pre-folded diapers and strongly recommend that you do too. They are called Diaper Service Quality pre-folded diapers. They are great, wear well and last a long time! I think I paid $23.00 for one dozen. (I returned some disposable diapers that we received as a gift and used the money to buy the cloth.) I have about 5 dozen now but I got most of them for free (as gifts or from people who no longer needed theirs). I only purchased 1 dozen of the DSQ from a mail order place on the Net. They are out of business now but you can find them other places. Also look on E-bay. They often have them too.

One thing that makes my cloth diaper experience different from the horror stories your grandparents tell is that I use diaper liners. They are fast, cheap (about $3.50 per box) and easy. I cut them in half and use 1 for each diaper. One box of liners lasts me almost 1 year. I have found them at Babies R Us and E-bay.

I use good diaper pins that I purchased from the diaper seller and I stick the pins into a bar of soap or beeswax when not in use so they pierce the diapers easier. (With good pins, I only poked the kids 3 times in 3 years. Mike never poked them at all!)

I use plastic pants that button up on the sides. I also purchased those mail order. I use the Alexis brand. They last MUCH and I do mean MUCH longer than the Gerber plastic pants you purchase at Wal-Mart or K-mart. I have about 5 pairs of each size. I don't use clean plastic pants every time I change a diaper. If the plastic pants are only wet, I put them right back on. There is not usually enough to make the diaper wet and the plastic pants generally aren't wet on the outside either.

I made 2 diaper pail liners out of rain ponchos by sewing up the sides. I put those in a kitchen trash can with a lid that closes. I just throw the wet diapers and liners into the pail with nothing in it. I don't soak my diapers. I dump the poop and the liners in the toilet. (Much easier than grandma's method!) I reuse the liners that were only wet after they are washed and dried with the diapers. They wash well so I get several uses out of them which saves even more. I don't dunk the diapers in the toilet unless they are REALLY bad. I have done it maybe 5 times in almost 3 years with 2 kids. In order to avoid directly handling the soiled diapers, I put the opening of the diaper pail bag into the open washer, then turn the bag inside out to empty the diapers into the washer. I throw the entire bag into the washer inside out to wash with the diapers.

Instead of using disposable wipes, I use small rag wash cloths (old wash cloths cut in half). They have more traction and do a better job of cleaning than disposable wipes. Where I use one wash cloth, I might have to use four or five of the disposable wipes. I do still use disposable wipes for traveling, but I save a lot by not using them every day.

I wash diapers about every two or three days. Washing this frequently really keeps them from smelling. (Unlike wine, diapers do NOT improve with age! ;-) Every time I wash, I wash with vinegar and detergent. The vinegar works wonders removing the urine smell and also keeps the house from stinking while I do laundry. I put diapers through the rinse cycle twice. Then I dry them on the line or dryer depending on the time of year. (Diapers last much longer when dried on a clothes line and the sun helps keep then white. They wear out much faster if you always use the dryer.) I use bleach about every 1 or 2 weeks to keep them white in the winter when I can't line-dry them.

If I were to buy disposables I would spend about $350 a year per child for diapers, wipes and extra trash bags. (Many people have said they use double that at least.) I only spent about $50 for the trash can, rain ponchos and plastic pants and $23.00 for one dozen diapers. I spend about .50 a load to wash them. (approx. $65 per year. This didn't change when I had two in cloth vs. one in cloth.) With one child in diapers for 2 1/2 years and one for 2 years I saved over $855 in the 3 years that my kids were in diapers.

That's it. It's so easy and so cheap that I would rather spend that money on something else!

IS IT BETTER TO BE SINGLE OR MARRIED?

"Single is better, for the simple reason that I wouldn't want to change no diapers.

Of course, if I did get married, I would just phone my mother and have her come over for some coffee and diaper-changing."

From a 9-year old girl

Debt Free
Holidays

Valentine's Day On A Dime

Using a little imagination, you can make your Valentine's day a little more fun and a lot less expensive. If you want to add a little personalized romance or if you don't have the time or money to buy all the pre-made things in the store, here are some ideas to help you make the day special.

For The Kids:

* **My mom always made a great but inexpensive Valentine's Day treat for us.** She would take construction paper and cut a big heart out of it. (About 8x10 inches) then she would staple the edges together and write our names and an I love you on the outside. Then she would fill the heart with candy, purchased on clearance after Christmas. It was very inexpensive but we loved it!

* **Do a Valentine's treasure hunt.** Leave little notes around with the last one leading back to the kitchen table with a heart full of candy.

For The Lunches:

* **Make heart shaped Valentine's cookies,** cut the kids (or hubby's) sandwiches with a heart shaped cookie cutter to make a heart sandwich. Add a few Valentine's chocolates and put a note in red with a big heart on their napkin.

* **Serve anything red for the day.** Serve red Jello, red pudding, red apples, toast with strawberry jelly, tomato soup, red applesauce, red Kool-aid, strawberry milk, or red frosted cookies. Use powered food coloring from the cake store to get the deepest shade of red. Leave sticks of red gum in their Valentine's Day cards.

* **Make red heart shaped cupcakes.** Make cupcakes as usual but place a marble down the side of the muffin tin between the muffin tin and each cupcake cup. This will make heart shaped cupcakes.

* **Make hearts out of chocolate chips** in each of your pancakes.

164

Things To Do With Or For Your Honey:

* **Mail your pre-addressed and stamped Valentines to Loveland,** Colorado and they will postmark them and mail them for you. Send them to: Postmaster, Attn: Valentines, Loveland, CO 80537

* **Make a treasure hunt for your spouse.** Start by mailing or e-mailing him the first clue. Then leave clues all over the house, yard, car or his office telling him where to find the next clue. End the hunt by making a picnic in the back yard or going to a park for a picnic. Use your imagination and have fun. The simple things are the ones people remember.

* **Go to a bookstore and enjoy the silence and browse.** Get a cup of coffee and make a date of it.

* **Celebrate Valentine's day AFTER Valentine's day.** Everything is half off.

* **Mail a love letter to your hubby's work.**

* **Send your spouse a sexy email message.**

* **Leave "Why I love you" messages all over the house.** Buy a package of the cheap Valentines. Leave a message on each one and hide them all over the house for your honey. They will get to enjoy the gift for months!

* **Use lipstick to make hearts and love notes on the rear view mirror,** car windows, bathroom mirror or windows of the house. Leave a kiss on his napkin for lunch or dinner.

* **Make a bunch of hearts out of construction paper.** Put a love note on each one. Paste them all over the front door or car before your hubby or kids come home from work.

* **If you don't have money to go out,** have a picnic on the floor. Use some candles and lay a soft blanket on the floor. Put on some soft music and have a romantic Valentine's dinner on the floor. Use some white Christmas lights for additional romantic lighting!

Poetry On A Plate!

The $6 Gourmet Valentine's Dinner for Two

For under $6, you can make a special Valentine's Day dinner for two.
Tawra and her mom have put together this Valentine menu that is sure to please that special someone!

You can add a little romantic ambiance with a nice place setting.
Fancy napkins, tapered candles, china place settings and a lace tablecloth add a nice touch. It is relatively easy to find one or two nice settings of china for 50 cents each at thrift stores or garage sales.

If you happened to hit the after Christmas sales, you may have found that white taper candles usually get marked down 75% after the holidays. You can also purchase red napkins, lace tablecloths, and red ribbon after Christmas for .50 - $1.00. Try it after next Christmas. You can also purchase things on sale 50% after Valentine's Day and keep them for next year. ... Of course if you're with the one you love, who needs food for Valentine's Day!

For The Menu: ($5.69 for 2 people)
French Onion Soup
Tomato Basil Salad
Maple-Glazed Chicken
Glazed Carrots
Lemon Potatoes
Red Velvet Cake
Water with lemon slices
Tea or coffee with dessert

French Onion Soup ($1.15)
2 onions, thinly sliced (yellow onions work best) (.25)
2 Tbsp. butter or margarine (.10)
2 cups beef stock (made with bullion cubes or beef bones) (.10)
1 bay leaf
2 slices day-old French bread (.20)
1/2 cup mozzarella or Swiss cheese, grated (.50)

Melt butter in a skillet. Sautee onions until slightly brown. Add onions to beef broth in saucepan. Simmer slowly 10 minutes or simmer overnight in the crock pot on low. Pour into bowls. Place bread on top of each bowl of soup, and sprinkle the cheese on top. Then set under broiler and cook until cheese is melted and brown.

Tomato Basil Salad ($1.44)
4 large peeled tomatoes (.79)
Salt and pepper (to taste)
1 Tbsp. wine vinegar (.10)
2 Tbsp. olive oil (.05)
1/3 cup fresh basil leaves, chopped into small pieces (.50)

Dice tomatoes and combine with salt, pepper, vinegar, oil and basil. Serve. You may also add cubes of mozzarella cheese.

Maple-Glazed Chicken ($1.43)
1/4 cup maple syrup (.05)
4 tsp. lemon juice (.05)
1 Tbsp. butter or margarine (.05)
Salt and pepper (to taste)
4 pieces chicken ($1.28 purchased on sale at $1.34/.lb)

Preheat oven to 450°. Mix maple syrup, lemon juice and butter together in a small saucepan. Simmer 5 minutes. Spray a baking dish and place chicken in it. Add salt and pepper to the chicken. Bake 10 minutes. Remove chicken from oven and pour on glaze. Bake 15 minutes more or until juices run clear.

Glazed Carrots (.37)
1/2 lb. fresh carrots or baby carrots (.12)
1/2 stick margarine (.05)
6 Tbsp. brown sugar (.10)
1 tsp. cinnamon (.05)
1 tsp. ginger (optional) (.05)

Clean carrots and cut into bite-size pieces. Steam 10 minutes in a small amount of boiling water (just until tender). Melt margarine in a large skillet over low heat. Add brown sugar, cinnamon and ginger. Cook 1-2 minutes. Add hot carrots, stirring well to coat. Remove when shiny and well glazed.

Lemon Potatoes (.75)
6 new potatoes or 2 medium potatoes, cut in halves or quarters (.50)
2 Tbsp. margarine (.05)
1/2 tsp. lemon peel, grated
1 1/2 tsp. lemon juice (.05)
1 tsp. chives, chopped (.10)
1/4 tsp. salt
dash of pepper
dash of nutmeg (.05 for all spices)

Clean and steam potatoes 20 minutes (until tender). Heat remaining ingredients just to boiling. Pour lemon butter over potatoes and serve.

Red Velvet Cake (.50 for 2 servings)*
3/4 cup butter
2 eggs
1 1/2 cups sugar
1 1/2 tsp. cocoa
1/4 tsp. salt
1 tsp. baking soda
2 tsp. vinegar
2 tsp. vanilla
1-2 oz. red food coloring
2 1/2 cups flour
1 cup buttermilk

Cream together butter, eggs and sugar in a bowl. Add the rest of the ingredients except the flour and buttermilk. Mix well. Add flour and buttermilk alternately. Beat until all the lumps are out. Pour into a greased and floured 9x13 inch pan. Bake at 350° for 30 minutes or until a tooth pick inserted in the center comes out clean. Frost with Red Velvet Frosting.

Red Velvet Frosting
2/3 cup milk
1/2 cup flour
1/2 cup butter
1/2 cup sugar
1 tsp. vanilla

Cook milk and flour until thick, stirring constantly. Cool thoroughly. Beat milk and flour for one minute until fluffy. Beat butter and sugar until creamy. Add to milk and flour and add vanilla. Mix well. Frosts one Red Velvet Cake.

*Or purchase a box mix on sale .79 and canned frosting on sale .69. plus .50 for eggs, etc. to make the cake $1.48

Easter Egg-Stravaganza

OK, so the kids noticed on the calendar that Easter is approaching and they want to make a huge production of dying eggs. In the past, the little stickers you bought at the store sufficed, but now they want the real thing. Here are some old standards with a few new ideas for you.

One important note: When the kids get really excited about egg dying, don't feel sorry for them and pour the left over egg dye in their bath water so they can have more fun (no matter how much they beg and plead! Especially if it's food coloring). Someone might panic and declare a citywide medical quarantine if they see your kids dyed all sorts of strange colors in their Easter finery.

Before you decorate Easter eggs, cover the entire table with newspaper. Keep a huge roll of paper towels or rags handy for messes. Have each kid wear one of dad's old (now disposable) tee shirts.

Making Easter Egg Stands
Cut toilet paper roll cores into one inch cylinders and use for egg stands. Decorate with stickers or paint.

Decorating Eggs

Traditional Method

Hard boil eggs. Fill several mugs with boiling water and add 1-2 tsp. vinegar. Place a few drops of desired food coloring in each mug. Place eggs in mugs for several minutes until eggs reach desired shades.

Remove with a spoon. Place on paper towel to dry. When dry, polish with a small amount of shortening on a paper towel. Buff until glossy.

You can draw or write on the eggs with a light colored or white crayon before dipping. The drawing will remain white after the egg is dipped.

To clean out mugs, put a little bleach water in the cups and soak for a few minutes.

Natural Easter Egg Dyes

If you would like to try dying eggs naturally, try the following:
* **Yellow--** yellow onion skins, turmeric (1/2 tsp. per cup water) celery leaves
* **Orange**--any yellow dye plus beet juice
* **Red**--beets, paprika, red onion skins
* **Pink**--cranberry juice
* **Blue**--blackberries, grape juice concentrate, red cabbage
* **Brown**--black tea, white oak, juniper berry, coffee, barberry
* **Light purple**--blackberries, grapes, violets
* **Green**--alfalfa, spinach, kale, violet blossom plus 1/4 tsp. baking soda, tansy, nettle, chervil, sorrel, parsley, carrot tops, beet tops or dip yellow egg in blue dye

Hard boil eggs with 1 tsp. vinegar in the water. Place dying ingredients in non-aluminum pans, cover with water and boil 5 minutes to 1 hour until desired color is achieved. Use enough material to make at least 1 cup dye. Crush ingredients as they boil to extract as much dye as possible. Strain the dye. Most dyes should be used hot. Let each egg sit in the dye until it reaches the desired color. Some dyes will take longer than others to make the desired colored on the egg. Remove the egg and let dry.

Glitter Eggs - Place 1 tablespoon each of glue and water in a cup. Stir the mixture and then paint the eggs with it. Sprinkle with glitter. This can also add sparkle to already dyed eggs!

Decoupaged Eggs - Tear small pieces of wrapping paper, napkins, stickers, or clip art. Mix equal amounts of glue and water. Paint egg with glue mixture. Place paper on top and then cover with more glue mixture. Let dry.

Waxed Eggs - Dip a portion of the eggs in melted paraffin or candle wax. Then dip them in the dye. Remove from dye. Dry and peel off the wax. The egg will be white on one half and colored on the other half. You can also dip in dye before waxing to get two colors.

Hollow Eggs - Poke a hole in one end of an egg with a very small needle. Poke another slightly larger hole in the other end. Then blow on the small end and the egg will come out the other side. Decorate as desired.

Easter Basket Ideas

A reader asks: **Got any inexpensive ideas for Easter gifts for the kids?** Also, do you have any ideas that would focus on the real meaning of Easter and not just bunnies and eggs?

Tawra: **Easter is a great time of the year to celebrate,** especially if you have the hope that comes from Jesus Christ and His resurrection. Here are some ideas for Easter gifts. Try some of them and if the creative juices start flowing, make up some of your own!

Easter Baskets:
You can find inexpensive Easter baskets at garage sales and thrift stores. I never spend more than .25 for one.

If you don't have Easter baskets, you can also use:

* Plain wicker baskets
* Baskets spray painted an Easter color
* A cute straw hat
* A pail for the sandbox
* A bowl wrapped in tissue paper
* Paper sacks that the kids decorate. Cut out pictures from magazines or use stickers. Glue or stick them on and then paint or color around them.
* Any sort of plastic storage container. These often can be used later for storage.
* For a "family" Easter basket, set a nice plate on the table with Easter grass and goodies arranged on the plate or platter. This is great when you have older kids.

Fillers for Easter Baskets:

* **Buy candy after Valentine's Day** at half price and keep to fill Easter baskets.

* **Make Easter cookies** in the shapes of bunnies, eggs, crosses or any other Easter shape that comes to mind and decorate.

* **Popcorn Balls or Rice Krispie** treats colored in pastel colors.

* **String fruit loops** onto yarn and tie to make a necklace.

* **Do not fill baskets,** but instead put jelly beans and candy in plastic eggs so the kids can fill their own baskets. You can also put nickels, dimes, toy soldiers, bugs, stickers, barrettes or hair ribbons in the eggs. Hide them outside or in the house if you live in a climate where it's usually cold on Easter.

* **Make coupons for getting out of chores,** staying up late one night, having a friend over for a sleep over or a special dinner they like.

* **Like new books** purchased at garage sales or thrift stores.

* **Homemade slime,** play dough, sidewalk chalk, bubbles or the ingredients for crystal gardens.

* **Wacky crayons** Crayon pieces melted together in a muffin tin to make a "big" crayon.

* **Flower seeds** that the kids can grow

* **Mini-stuffed animals** purchased at garage sales or on clearance the year before.

* **Paper dolls or coloring books.** There are many available on the Internet that you can print yourself.

* **For teenagers,** put these items in baskets: lotions, soaps, suntan lotions, fingernail polish, movie tickets, tickets for getting out of a chore, ticket for $5 worth of car gas, clothes purchased on clearance and of course lots of candy!

* **Leave a trail of jelly beans** or candy kisses from their room to their Easter basket.

* Easter Kisses

Put some Hershey Kisses or chocolate chips in a plastic bag and attach the following poem:

This cute little bunny has hopped all day
Been delivering baskets for the holiday.
His paws are so tired and his little nose itches.
He left you something special—something to fill all your wishes.
These cute little hugs and Easter kisses.

* Put 1 Pound Jelly Beans into a bag, and attach this poem:

RED is for the blood He gave.
GREEN is for the grass He made.
YELLOW is for the sun so bright.
ORANGE is for the edge of night.
BLACK is for the sins we made.
WHITE is for the grace he gave.
PURPLE is for His hour of sorrow.
PINK is for our new tomorrow.
A bag full of jelly beans colorful and sweet,
Is a prayer, is a promise, is a special treat.

* Easter Carrot Treats

Buy disposable plastic decorating bags and fill them with orange jellybeans or cheese balls. Then stick some green Easter grass in the top of the bag (leave some hanging out) and secure the bag with a rubber band and then ribbon so that it resembles a carrot.

Resurrection Eggs

* 1 dozen plastic Easter eggs
* 1 egg carton
* construction paper

Decorate the top of the carton with construction paper and any other decoration that seems fitting.

Fill each egg with the item listed in parenthesis below, along with a piece of paper containing the listed verse. For example the first egg will have a piece of bread along with verse #1 accompanying the bread below. Put them in order in the carton so you remember which number is which.

Once you have made the Resurrection Eggs, you can decide the method you want to use to open them. You might open one per day during the twelve days before Easter or if you're having a big family get-together, you may choose to open them then. It is also fun for the kids to do this the day you decorate Easter eggs with them.

1. (Bread) Matthew 26:26
While they were eating Jesus took a piece of bread, gave a prayer of thanks, broke it, and gave it to His disciples. "Take and eat it," He said, "This is My body."

2. (Coins) Matthew 26: 14-15
Then one of the twelve disciples, named Judas Iscariot, went to the chief priests and asked, "What will you give me if I betray Jesus to you?" They counted out thirty silver coins and gave them to him.

3. (Purple cloth, representing a purple robe) Mark 15:17
They put a purple robe on Jesus. . .

4. (Thorns, like on a rose stem) Matthew 27:29
Then they made a crown out of thorny branches and placed it on His head, and put a stick on His right hand; then they knelt before Him and made fun of Him. "Long live the King, of the Jews!" they said.

5. (Scourge-a small piece of rope or thick string) Mark 15:15
Pilate wanted to please the crowd, so he set Barabbas free for
them. Then he had Jesus whipped and handed Him over to be
crucified.

6. (Small cross) John 19: 17-18a
He went out, carrying His cross, and came to "The Place of the
Skull," as it is called. (In Hebrew it is called "Golgotha.") There
they crucified Him.

7. (Nails) John 20:25b
Thomas said to them, "Unless I see the scars of the nails in His
hands and put my finger on those scars and my hand in His
side, I will not believe."

8. (Sign saying "THIS IS THE KING OF THE JEWS.") Luke 23:38
Above Him were written these words: THIS IS THE KING OF
THE JEWS.

9. (Small piece of sponge) Matthew 27:48
One of them ran up at once, took a sponge, soaked it in cheap
wine, put it on the end of a stick, and tried to make Him drink it.

10. (Something representing a spear (i.e. a toothpick)) John 19:34
One of the soldiers plunged his spear into Jesus' side, and at
once blood and water poured out.

11. (Rock) Matthew 27:59-60
Joseph took the body, wrapped it in a new linen sheet, and
placed it in his own new tomb, which he had just recently dug
out of solid rock. Then he rolled a large stone across the
entrance to the tomb and went away.

12. (Empty) Matthew 28:6
He is not here He has risen just as He said.

Bunnies And Ham And Eggs, OH MY!!

It's almost that time of year again. You're standing, dumbfounded, in front of a mound of hard boiled eggs, sliced ham and chocolate Easter bunnies. You wonder "what am I going to do with 6 dozen eggs, 6 lbs. of ham and 25 chocolate bunnies". The stress of it is almost enough to send you to bed for a week--or at least tear most of your hair out. Here are a few ideas and recipes to help you avoid both of those.

First the bunnies:

Take a rolling pin and crush the life out of them. Then use the crumbs to:

* Sprinkle on ice cream
* Use in milk shakes
* Stir a few in a mug of hot chocolate
* Use in place of chocolate chips for making cookies
* Melt for dipping fruit and candy
* If your kids didn't receive an excess of bunnies this year, buy solid bunnies after Easter on Clearance and use in place of chocolate chips for baking. You can usually get them for 1/4 the price of chocolate chips.

Next the eggs:

* Deviled eggs
* Slice them on tossed salad
* Egg Salad
* Golden Morning Sunshine

If you're wondering how to cook a delicious Easter Ham here is an easy recipe:

Spiced Honey Ham

1 ham	¼ cup honey
½ cup mustard	¼ cup orange juice
½ cup brown sugar	1 tsp. cloves

Cover the bottom of a roasting pan with aluminum foil. Bake ham at 250° for 1 hour. Reduce the heat to 200° and roast another 10 hours.
Mix the rest of the ingredients. Score the top of ham. Pour mixture over ham and begin basting the ham 3 hours before serving. Baste every half hour or so with ham juices.

This is great because you can put in the oven overnight and it will be ready the next day for the noon meal. The cooking time can go for longer if needed to fit your schedule, since it is at such a low temperature.
Serves 4-6.

Use the extra ham:

* Diced in omelets and chef salads
* Added to Golden Morning Sunshine
* Sliced thin for sandwiches
* Cubed ham with cubed fruit such as Mandarin oranges, pineapple, bananas, strawberries or kiwi on skewers to make fruit kabobs.
* Top a tortilla with ham, salsa, and cheddar cheese and warm, for a hot ham and cheese sandwich.
* Save bone for bean or split pea soup.
* Ham and Noodles
* Ham and Potatoes
* Ham Casserole
* Ham Salad

Chop ham and freeze to use in:

Potato salad	Scalloped potatoes,
Green beans	Au gratin potatoes,
Scrambled eggs	Pasties
Omelets	Pizza (with pineapple)
Potato soup	Top baked potatoes.

Deviled Eggs
6 hard boiled eggs
1/8 tsp. salt
1/4 tsp. prepared mustard
1/3 cup mayonnaise
1 tsp. vinegar (optional)
paprika
parsley, chopped

Shell hard boiled eggs and cut in half. Remove yolks and mash; add remaining ingredients and mix until smooth. Heap into whites and sprinkle with paprika or chopped parsley.

Garlic Deviled Eggs
Add 1 clove garlic, pressed to deviled eggs.

Egg Salad
6 hard boiled eggs, chopped
1/2 cup mayonnaise or salad dressing
1 small stalk celery, chopped
1 small onion, chopped, or 1 tsp. onion powder
1/4 tsp. salt
1/4 tsp. pepper

Mix all ingredients. Best if chilled for 1 or 2 hours. Makes 4 sandwiches.

Golden Morning Sunshine
(You can use more or less sauce and eggs to taste)

2 cups white sauce
4 eggs, hard boiled and chopped

Make white sauce. Once the white sauce has thickened, add eggs. Serve on toast.

White Sauce

2 cups milk
4 Tbsp. flour
dash salt
2 Tbsp. margarine

In a jar mix milk and flour. Shake well. Melt margarine in a 1 quart sauce pan. Stir in flour-milk mixture and cook over low heat until mixture thickens and starts to bubble. Keep stirring until thickened completely. Makes 2 cup.

Ham and Potatoes
6 potatoes, peeled and thinly sliced
2 cups cheddar cheese, shredded
1/2 -1 lb. ham, thinly sliced
1 onion, chopped
1 can (10 3/4 oz.) cream of mushroom soup

Layer the potatoes, then some cheese, then some ham and then chopped onion. Continue to layer to 3 inches from top of crockpot. Then pour cream of mushroom soup on top. Let simmer for several hours on low until potatoes are cooked through.

Ham Casserole

1 lb. noodles, cooked
1-1 1/2 cups ham, cooked and cubed
1 tsp. salt
3/4 cup peas, drained and cooked
2 cups white sauce
1 bouillon cube

Add ham and peas to cooked noodles. Dissolve bouillon into 1/4 cup boiling water. Mix the bouillon and salt in the white sauce. Bake covered at 300° for 20-30 minutes.
*12 oz. of tuna may be used in place of ham.

Sheala's Ham and Noodles

8 oz. pkg. egg noodles, cooked
1/2 lb. ham
1 can (10 3/4 oz.) cream of chicken soup
1 cup cheddar cheese, grated

Mix first three ingredients together in a casserole dish and bake at 350° for 20 minutes until warmed. Top with cheese and bake an additional 5 minutes or until cheese melts.

Ham Salad

leftover ham
hard boiled eggs
mayonnaise
mustard

Grind ham and eggs in a meat grinder. Moisten with mayonnaise and small amount of mustard (approximately 1 Tbsp. for an entire ham). Serve on bread or toast.

Be Creative With Halloween Decorations!

I just stepped outside and took a deep breath and then another one and another one. No I don't have a breathing problem or anything. It's just that for the first time in months, I don't feel like I'm breathing in an aquarium. (We live in Kansas with very high humidity) The air is crisp and cool and that means fall is here.

At one point in our lives, that would have been the signal for us to haul out boxes and sacks full of Halloween decorations and go to work. It would usually take us at least a month to put everything out. We were one of those families who would put out a "monstrous" (Ha! Ha! No pun intended) display. We literally had hundreds of people drive by our home just to see our decorations. It really was a lot of work, especially because back then you couldn't buy much to use for outside Halloween decorations. We had to use our imagination and make our own.

We like to have fun at Halloween and not scare the wits out of everyone, so we try to keep our decorations cute and funny looking. To us, Halloween is a time for children to dress up and for one night a year be what they always dreamed of being, whether it's a fairy princess, a ballerina, Superman or even a robot. They get to be on the "stage" for one night to show everyone how beautiful, strong or funny they look. And to end a perfect night they get tons of candy, bags of candy and did I mention, a whole bunch of candy??

Here are some ideas of things we did to have a whole lot of fun for very little money. You can use these same basic principles for any holiday decorating.

1. You don't have to have a lot of decorations for your display to look nice. I drive by one home every year and each season the owners put out one simple something. For example, in the summer they have one beautiful pot of flowers sitting on their porch. In the fall a pot of mums, for Halloween, one pumpkin with a smiley face and at Christmas one pretty lit up wreath on the door. It's never a lot, but I always get pleasure when I drive by the place and see their one simple decoration.

2. We work all year buying things at garage sales or thrift stores for our decorations. We started out with about 25 plastic pumpkins to set out for a pumpkin patch. The next year we added another 50 and drilled holes in the bottoms so we could put lights in them. After a few years we had 200-300 of them that we had collected. We never paid more then 5-10 cents for them. If you want to have a big display, start small and just add a little bit more to your decorations each year.

3. Cute homemade decorations make Halloween fun! If you see something in a magazine or somewhere that you think is cute but too expensive, try to copy it and make it yourself:

* **I saw a cute rake in a magazine that I loved.** It was an old rake that had a few silk flowers tied on it and a sign that said "Free leaves, rake all you want." I just happened to have a dead 50 year old rake in my shed I was going to throw away, so I pulled it out, found an old board and some paint (I could have used a marker too), painted on the words and tied on a couple of stray silk flowers that I had and voila! I had a cute rake and saved about $25.

* **It takes nothing to stuff some old clothes with plastic bags** and make a scarecrow family.

* **If you are a little handy,** put your talent to good use. My husband took and old metal trash can and motorized it so that the lid moved up and down and when it opened it popped out a Sylvester the cat.

4. We found decorations in unusual places. Once we went to the grocery store where they had a gigantic pumpkin. The thing was about 8-10 feet across. We asked the manager it they threw it out at the end of the season and he said no. We told him what we needed it for and discovered that he had seen our display and liked it. He said "Come by on Halloween morning and you can take it to use and then bring it back." It doesn't ever hurt to ask about anything. Most people aren't mean and hateful, but are usually kind and helpful.

5. Get more bang for your buck. Buy things that have a big impact but cost little. A couple of bags of spider webs and plastic spiders can cover a lot of area and look "cool" but cost very little. I use spider webs for everything. They're great to use to cover throw pillows for a party, put in your hair, hang on the lights or wrap around the handles of silverware. You just can't have too much.

6. Use what you already have around the house.

  * **We were having a Halloween party and to add to the effect,** we dug out some black sheets and covered all the furniture. It changed the whole look of the room.

  * **Another year, my husband found some 10 foot long, thin metal rods.** We stuck them in the ground, added Styrofoam wig heads to each one and hung some large pieces of sheer fabric I had gotten for free from a friend over the tops of the heads. Everyone loved them. The sheer material had a much more realistic see through look then just a sheet. At night, you couldn't see the rod so it looked like these ghosts were floating 10 feet up in the air.

7. Start the day after Halloween to prepare for next year. If your kids get a bunch of plastic spiders when they go trick or treating, save them and add them to the decoration box. If your child dressed as a pumpkin this year, save the costume, stuff it next year and set it out with the decorations. Try to think of ways to incorporate any old costumes into your decorations.

KITCHEN CRY

Howard came home from work one evening and there was his wife Miriam in the kitchen crying out loud.

"What's the matter, darling?" he asked her.

"I just don't know what to do," said Miriam. "Because we were eating in for a change, I cooked us a special dinner - but the dog has just eaten it."

"Don't worry," said Howard, "I'll get us another dog."

$25 Halloween Party

Halloween is one of our favorite holidays. Last year we decided to have a Halloween party for my brother's family, my mom and my family. We had 10 people, including five adults, four kids and a baby. We were able to put it together for less than $25 for the decorations, food, party treats and costumes for my family.

Keep in mind when reading about what we did that we save a lot of money by using items we already have, adapting them if necessary and buying only the minimum necessary from discount or dollar stores. A little creativity goes a long way for any holiday preparation and the kids always seem to look back the most fondly on the things that cost the least but required a little more thought. Usually, if you pay more for decorations, you are buying someone else's creativity and it will be less memorable.

Here is what we did and a break down of the prices:

Decorations

Purchased on clearance the year before:

Spider webs- 3 large ones (.60), 10 small, ($1.00)

10 Spider Rings- (.20)- Placed all over the table

Large black spider web- (.50)

Streamers- purchased from Dollar Tree ($1.00)

Happy Halloween Banner- (Free had for years)

Table Cloth- (Free) We had this one that Mike's folks gave us years ago. A black sheet could be used also.

Balloons- (.25) from a garage sale

Candles (Free) We already had them.

Decorations

We draped spider webs from the ceiling fan to each wall and hung streamers all over the room. We turned the pictures so they were crooked or falling down. I didn't dust for a month. We had another large black spider web that we hung on the wall.

We draped a black sheet over the couch. We reused a sheet that we had purchased for $2.00 at a discount store and previously used for a craft show. We lit as many candles as we could find (15-20) and placed them in various spots around the room.

We set the table with a table cloth and cups, plates and napkins- (.50 for all) purchased new at a garage sale. We laid vinyl gloves next to each plate. (I already had a huge package from another project.) We didn't allow anyone to use any utensils to eat. They could only eat with their hands. We drew pumpkin faces with permanent marker on the orange plates.

We laid out tags to identify the food that I made using clip art and a spooky font. Then we tore out the tags and spread tea all over them to make them look old. Some of the names were Witches Brew, Slime, Vomit, Monster Toes, Deviled Eyeballs, Floating Eyeballs, Octopus etc.

Food

Octopus- Hot dogs, chili and cheese to go with the hot dogs. ($2.50)

Monster toes $.25 (used a full package of hot dogs between the monster toes and octopus)

Slime- Lime Jello (.30)

Graveyard pudding ($1.50)

Vomit- Salsa (.25)

Tortilla Chips ($2.00)

Cupcakes with spider webs and spiders on top. ($1.50 *Cupcake liners were .10 on clearance)

Ghost Suckers (.40)

Caramel apples ($1.50 for caramels and apples)

Punch ($1.00)

Deviled eyeballs (.50 Deviled eggs with an olive in the center.)

Floating eyeballs- Green olives floating in water. (.50)

Orange Popcorn Balls (.75)
We put the food on either silver platters or clear bowls so that you could see the full effect of the food.

Costumes

We were able to do costumes for our family of 5 around $2.00.

I was a witch. (A costume I have had for years. ☺) $0

BJ and David were both Superman. ($0) They wore some Superman pajama's that they received as a present from their uncle Dave who thinks he is Superman. ☺ We then put red hair gel in their hair and spiked it. The gel was free from a rebate.

Mike was Kryptonite Man. (.20) (You know like Kryptonite that makes Superman lose his power.) He wore a green shirt, put a green blanket around him and made a Superman like logo on the computer to wear on his chest. Then we colored his hair and face green with face paint. The .20 was for the face paint. He put a giant green and black spider on his shoulder. (one we had had for years and originally got for something like .10 at a garage sale).

Elly was a princess Barbie. We got the head piece and jewelry at the dollar store for $1.00. She wore a regular pair of her dress shoes and her dress cost $0.25 from a garage sale.

Two Trick or Treat bags (.60)

Games

Pumpkin carving and painting. $1.00 for the paints and carving supplies.

Halloween treasure hunt. Click this link for what the clues said. ($5.00 for the small toys and treats. This was for the 4 kids)

Sidewalk chalk- drawing on the driveway with glow in the dark sidewalk chalk. ("Nan" gave it as a gift to the kids.)

Then we went Trick or Treating.

We didn't plan too many games. The kids were in school all day and trick or treating started about 6:30 so we only planned enough games to last from when the kids got out of school until we went trick or treating. If you're not sure, plan for extra games and then drop some of them if you run out of time. Don't feel like you have to do it just because you planned it.

We had a blast for $24.35!

You can have great parties for very little money. Just try to think of different uses for things you already have. Try shopping you local dollar store. Many of them have lots of great stuff for very little money. Be sure and purchase items for next year's party on clearance. One of the ways we save a bundle is planning at clearance time for the next year. You can also buy extra face paint, hair gels etc. for birthday parties or school carnivals! Just because you're frugal doesn't mean you can't have fun!

Great Costumes for Less!

You can really come up with some cute and clever ideas for costumes, even if you don't feel particularly creative. Don't wait until the night before Halloween to start your costumes. Look at the people and things around you and ask yourself how " how can I recreate this?" Look at thrift stores and garage sales for costumes. Go ahead and buy the costume or piece of a costume if the price is right. You really can't go wrong spending $0.25 on a piece of costume. Even if it doesn't work you haven't lost much.

Costumes can be very simple and still make a big impact. For example, instead of the usual witch robes, drag out your elegant black dress and add a witch hat with a veil of spider webbing stretched over your face. Cover the spider web with plastic spiders. For a man, a nice suit and tie and a funny mask makes a good simple costume. For a couple: get a REALLY big sweatshirt, both of you get in it and be Siamese twins! Some examples of costumes for kids are:

Sunflower - For the body, use a white sleeper or sweat suit. Paint the child's face yellow, adding black spots to simulate seeds if you like. Make a flower to fit on the child's head out of felt or glue sunflowers on a white hat.

Angel - Again use a white sweat suit or long white dress for the body. Make wings out of heavy white poster board and paint the edges gold. Attach tie straps to them that go around the shoulders. You can also shape a metal clothes hanger into a wing. Make two wings, hot glue fabric around them and add straps.

Pea Pod - Cut 2 small foam balls in half with an electric knife or a knife with a serrated blade. (Note: Do this BEFORE attaching them to the child!) Wrap in green fabric and pin them to the front of a green sweat suit. Make a hat out of 2 shades of green felt and a little brown felt for a stem.

Lion - Buy a yellow hat or dye a white hat yellow. Buy long brown fake fur, yellow fake fur and a yellow sweat suit. You can get fake fur at your favorite fabric store. Add brown fur to the top of the hat (for a mane), hot-glue yellow fur into a long tail, adding a poof of brown for the end. Pin the tail on the back of the costume. Make an oval of the fur for the child's tummy and use eyeliner for whiskers.

Dalmatian - Pin black felt dots onto a pair of white sweats. Paint black polka dots on the child's face. Add more polka dots to a white hat, make some black felt ears and add black shoes to finish it.

I Paint, Therefore I Am - Glue a copy of a painting with a face on it on a piece of cardboard. (Ex. Mona Lisa). Cut out the face and then put their face in instead.

Race Car Stroller - Decorate a stroller as a race car by adding fabric or paper racing stripes and a number. Add two flashlights for headlights, plus some reflector tape. If you want to get really creative, add a wind foil, a foil covered paper towel roller for an exhaust pipe or whatever else your clever mind conjures up. Cut a steering wheel out of cardboard for the child to hold. Your child can wear whatever clothes he wants. Just add an old helmet or baseball cap worn backwards.

Think of themes for all of the kids in the family.

It can be fun for all the kids to dress up in costumes that complement each other. Some sample themes are - superheroes, vegetables, candy bars, rabbit family (or other animals) or cartoon characters (i.e. Mickey Mouse, Minnie and Donald Duck). They could also dress in pairs like a mouse and cheese, a plant and a watering can or doctor and patient. The sky's the limit.

Christmas theme:
One child could go as a present, another a Christmas tree, another Rudolph and the 4th as Santa.

Ideas for how to make the costumes:

Rudolph - Dye an old pair of sweats brown. Put a light brown felt tummy on the shirt, make a set of cardboard antlers and paint the child's nose red.

Present - Wrap an old box that is big enough for the child to wear. Cut out the bottom of the box and make holes for the arms and head. The child can wear a turtleneck & stretch pants underneath it.

Christmas Tree - Cut two pieces of cardboard into the shape of a tree. Make two one for the front and one for the back. Hook them together with a piece of string over each shoulder. Paint the pieces green with latex paint and attach old tinsel and ornaments with hot glue. Make a star head piece by gluing glitter to a cardboard cutout or use a Christmas tree angel as a head piece.

Santa - Trim a pair of red sweats with white fake fur and a large black felt belt. Make a beard with more fake fur, top off with a Santa hat and add a little "Ho, Ho, Ho" for good measure.

Of course if all else fails you could wrap the child head to toe in aluminum foil and send him as a frozen burrito...

Having kids is like having a bowling alley installed in your brain.

- Martin Mull

Frighteningly Frugal Fun!

The average American family spends over $100 per year on Halloween goodies. As your kids drag you through aisles full of ghosts and goblins, the scariest thing about Halloween is threatening to leave bite marks in your pocketbook. No wonder so many moms flee screaming from the store... It can be much less expensive and a lot more fun to devise your own chilling creations. Here are a few tips that you can use to stave off the greenback gremlins and exercise your creative muscle. It won't hurt a bit!

Make-Up

Face Paint
1 tsp. corn starch
1/2 tsp. water
1/2 tsp. cold cream
food coloring
Mix all ingredients together in an old muffin pan and you are ready to paint. This amount makes one color.

Fake Wound
1 Tbsp Vaseline
tissue
cocoa powder
2-3 drops red food coloring

Place Vaseline in a bowl. Add food coloring. Blend with a toothpick. Stir in a pinch of cocoa to make a darker blood color. Separate tissue. Using 1 layer, tear a 2x3 inch piece and place at wound site. Cover with petroleum jelly and mold into the shape of a wound. The center should be lower than the sides. Fill the center with the red petroleum jelly mixture. Sprinkle center with some cocoa. Sprinkle a little around the edges of the wound to make darker.

Fake Blood- Mix 2/3 cup white corn syrup, 1 tsp. red food coloring, 2-3 drops blue food coloring to darken and 1 squirt dish soap (helps blood to run well).

Abrasions- Dab brown, red and black eye shadow on area. Apply blood over area with cotton balls. Use comb to gently scratch area in one direction. Apply cocoa or dirt over wound with cotton balls.

Black Eye- Apply red and blue eye shadow to depressions around eyes.

Bruises- Rub red and blue shadow over bony area to simulate recent bruises.
Blue and yellow eye shadow to create older bruises.

Look Old- Cover face with baby powder. Draw dark lines on your skin for wrinkles. Smooth edges to blend. Cover again with baby powder. Add baby powder to your hair to create gray hair.

Food

Deviled Eyeballs
Make deviled eggs. Add a green olive with pimento in the center for an "eyeball".

Radioactive Juice- Mix equal parts Mountain Dew and blue Kool-Aid

Toxic Juice- Add some green food coloring to lemonade for a spooky color!

Brains- Scramble eggs with some green, yellow and blue food coloring

Goblin Hand- Freeze green Kool-Aid in a rubber or latex glove, float in punch.

Edible Slime
Pour lime gelatin into a glass bowl. After it is partially set, add gummy worms. Chill until lightly set. Then serve slopped all over the plate.

Bloody Popcorn- Add red food color to melted butter and pour over popcorn.

Freeze gummy worms in ice cubes and add them to drinks. Cut gummy worms in half if needed.

Decorations

Use the tape from old cassettes or black yarn to make spider webs.

Use cotton balls stretched out for small spider webs.

Glass Jack-o-Lantern- Outline a pumpkin face on a spaghetti or pickle jar with black paint. The paint around the outside of it with orange paint. Place a candle inside for a jack-o-lantern.

Halloween Guess It Game

In this game, you challenge the participants to reach into mystery boxes filled with creepy things and try to guess what each item is. The person with the most correct answers wins the game. An example is if you want them to guess "grapes", you might try to confuse them by saying, "I think it's eyeballs..."

Cut a hole in the top of a shoe box or laundry box for each item to be used. Cover the box with black spray paint. Decorate each box with pumpkins or spiders for a more festive flavor.

Place the following items inside, one per box. Be sure to place enough of each item so the guests can adequately "feel" the guts.

Eyeballs- grapes or peeled cherry tomatoes
Intestines- Cooked Spaghetti
Skin- oil a piece of plastic bag
Brains- scrambled eggs
Hair- an old clown wig
Bones- thoroughly washed chicken bones placed in some sand
Vomit- chunky salsa
Fingers- hot dogs cut into finger sized pieces
Teeth- corn nuts, pine nuts or popcorn

Have a Pumpkin Hunt

Hide mini pumpkins like you would Easter Eggs. Let the kids find and decorate them. For small children use glue sticks with construction paper cut-outs for decorations.

Pumpkin Recycling

Peter Piper Picked a Profoundly Plump Pumpkin -- Now What does he do with it?

Every fall I get many questions about what to do with pumpkins.
Many people find curious fascination in imagining what it would be like to grow these versatile little gems, as if growing something that produces a large fruit is somehow more respectable than growing, say, a Serrano pepper. Many people eventually venture into pumpkin experimentation. Some succeed and many fail.

Much like a dog that chases a car, many people never give thought to what they would do if they actually succeeded in successfully raising a patch of these fall favorites. Whether you have found yourself with more pumpkins than you know what to do with or you are one of the people who had to buy pumpkins and duct tape them to the vine, these tips for roasting and using pumpkins are sure to help you make the most out of them (no matter how you acquired them)!

How To Roast A Pumpkin

You can only do this with a freshly carved pumpkin! Do not use on a pumpkin that has been carved and sitting out for several days.

To bake a fresh 6 to 7 pound pumpkin, halve the pumpkin crosswise and scoop out the seeds and strings. Place halves, hollow side down, in a large baking pan covered with aluminum foil and add a little water. Bake, uncovered, at 375° for 1 1/2 to 2 hours or until fork-tender. Remove. When cool, scrape pulp from shells and puree, a little at time, in food processor or blender. Mix with a little salt.

To freeze pumpkin puree. Put 1-2 cups in freezer bags along with spices and use in pies.

To use pumpkin puree for recipes: Line a strainer with a double layer of cheesecloth or a flour sack dish towel and let the pumpkin sit to drain out the extra moisture BEFORE cooking with it. Pumpkin is very moist, so in order for your recipe to come out correctly, you MUST strain it.

Roasted Pumpkin Seeds

Boil seeds in water for 5 minutes. Drain well. Sprinkle with salt or seasoned salt. Place a thin layer on a cookie sheet. Bake at 250°. Stir after 30 minutes. Bake 1/2-1 hour more or until crunchy.

*Squash seeds may also be used.

Why Ask Why?

Why is it that no plastic bag will open from the end on your first try?

How do those dead bugs get into those enclosed light fixtures?

Why is it that whenever you attempt to catch something that's falling off the table you always manage to knock something else over?

Less is More this Christmas!

After laying down my last women's magazine telling me how to be less stressed during the holidays, I'm even more confused and stressed then ever. On one page I'm told to take time for myself and indulge in a lovely spa bath. That sounds great, but I can hardly find time for a shower on a slow day in June let alone take a spa bath the week before Christmas.

As I turn the page, I'm told to give all my friends and family homemade ornaments to which I have lovingly glued 500 beads, each the size of a grain of sand. OK I'll admit I'm not a rocket scientist, but I am baffled when I try to imagine how I could accomplish these two things even if I didn't have an ever growing list of Christmas preparation tasks. Hmmm… Maybe I could lay in my spa bath carefully gluing on beads to ornaments throughout the night.

As I read on, there are articles telling me how not to gain weight at Christmas parties. Isn't that like telling a three year old to not get dirty while making mud pies? Oh! But it gets better. They then tell you to eat a meal before you go to the party. What? Is that some kind of new diet where you lose weight by eating two meals in the evening instead of one? If it is then I'm all for it. I mean really – who eats four carrot sticks and five pieces of celery at home then arrives at a party where they have pecan pie, five different types of fudge, 10 dozen cookies and egg nog and says "Oh no, I really couldn't eat a thing. I'm sooooo full..?" Excuse Me! Doesn't anyone live in the real world any more?

To top it all off (and the part I like the best) is after they tell us how to get rid of stress and not gain weight, they give us 10 pages of recipes for Christmas cookies made with real butter and cream that are decorated so elaborately in the pictures that it probably took a trained kitchen staff of 10 a week to make one cookie.

If you are like me and can't stand that kind of stress, try some of these Christmas ideas to help you have a relaxed and Merry Christmas:

Don't over-spend. It may be tempting to fixate yourself on the sparkling look in little Johnny's eye when he sees that $300 play car under the tree. **Advertising people are really good at feeding many parents' fantasies** of their children thinking that mom and dad are the peaches and cream for shelling out the cash and looking fondly back on the moment for the rest of their lives. The reality of it though is that most kids have lost all interest in that particular toy long before the credit cards are paid off.

When we were growing up, my mom pulled out all of the stops at Christmas to make it as wonderful for us as she possibly could. The funny thing is that now that we are grown, the things we remember the most fondly are mom's red Jello salad (made with red hots – yummy!) and sitting together and reading the Christmas story before opening our presents. I can't remember what presents I received, but I always look back on the Christmas story.

Do a few things well – Instead of trying to do everything and ending up depressed with how it all turns out, focus your energy on a couple of things that are the most important to you. You may be tempted to extravagantly decorate every room in your house, but if you don't have the time or energy, focus on one room, like a living or family room. If your entire house is beautiful but you have to go see a therapist when it's all over, the romantic mystique will be lost. Trust me, I know about this one from personal experience.

Limit activities – Don't commit to do too many things. One or two parties during the holiday season will make you get all tingly in that "It's a Wonderful Life" kind of way. One or two parties a week may send you over the edge, especially if you have kids. (Refer to my therapist comments above.)

This also applies to all of those appealing looking activities around town like Victorian Christmas events, Christmas celebrations at the zoo or winter carnivals. One or two can be a lot of fun, but too many will ruin the fun.

Limit cookie baking. Don't try to make 15 different kinds of cookies like Martha. She may look like she is super woman, but did you know she has a lot of people that help her? How much help do you get with your baking? I mean real help, not your five year old who makes everything twice as difficult for you. This is great for grandma, but you have to see your daughter every day and grandma can send her back when the house is sufficiently covered in flour. Again, pick your two or three top favorite cookies to bake and celebrate the fact that you had few enough priorities that you remembered to put the sugar in them.

Everything doesn't have to be homemade. I know that we advocate making your own stuff, but Marie Callendar's makes some great pies that you can pass off as homemade if you want to soothe your guilty Martha Stewart conscience. In 20 years, your kids will look fondly back on it as the best pie they ever had. But seriously, if you are making things homemade just to save money, remember that some things like candies and pies are often more expensive to make homemade, especially if you cut your finger while slicing the apples. Don't ask me how I know, just trust me on this one.

These aren't the only things you can do to reduce your stress, but if you stick to doing a few things well, you can truly relax and enjoy the season with your family. In the end, they would rather have fond memories of their time with you than memories of how strung out mom was after she burned the cookies.

My wife has a slight impediment in her speech. Every now and then she stops to breathe.

– Jimmy Durante

Holiday "To Do" List

The best way to relieve stress at the Holidays is not with a bubble bath (although they are fun) but by being organized. Even though I'm not normally a big list person, at Christmas I not only write a list but I write enough lists to fill a book (making up for my lack of lists the rest of the year ;-).

We wanted to create a cute calendar for readers that would list what you should do on each day, but every household is so different it was hard to put together something that would tell everyone when to do what and we didn't want to make anyone feel locked into a particular plan. It can almost be more stressful trying to follow someone else's plan then to have no plan at all.

So we came up with a compromise. It's a list of some general things that need to be done at Christmas. If you are attached to the calendar idea, take a calendar or day planner and, using this list, write down the day you want to get something done. For example on December 1, "Put up inside decorations."

If it is easier, simply hang the list by the calendar and then just mark things off as you do them. This is just a guide with our own hints and ideas. You can add to or take away from it as necessary.

The key to a low stress holiday season is to remember that the more you spread things out, the easier it will be. Doing just a few things each day is much easier than waiting for the last minute "Holiday Squeeze".

* **Make your list of all of the people who you plan to buy gifts,** including their sizes, things they would like and how much you can spend.

* **Make your list of the people you are sending Christmas cards** to and write the cards or at least get the envelopes addressed. You can then keep a few cards with you to write in during those "waiting minutes" when you're at the doctor, picking the kids up from school or on your break at work.

* **Get those sewing and craft projects done now!** (By Thanksgiving) Don't wait until Christmas Eve.

* **Decide on what cookies and candies you want to make.** Pull out the recipes now.

* **Decide on what you are going to have for holiday dinners.** Pull out the recipes.

* **Many types of cookies freeze well.** Mix up the dough several weeks ahead and freeze. That way all you have to do later is bake them.

* **For cookies that you can't freeze,** measure all the dry ingredients and put them in a plastic bag. I often do this three months early. Be sure to label the bag so you remember what is in it.

* **If you make your own pie crust,** make them ahead of time and freeze until you need them.

* **Several months ahead of time,** put a bag or container in the freezer and throw in those unused heels of bread or slices of dry bread to use for dressing.

* **If you make cornbread dressing,** make up your cornbread in early November and freeze.

* **Deep clean the house.**

* **Set up a wrapping table** or collect your wrapping things all together in one area so you can quickly and easily pull everything out to use. Wrap gifts as you buy them, not all at once at the last minute.

* **Make a list of linens and dishes that you will need for meals.**

* **Put up outside decorations.**

Christmas On A Budget!

Between high gas prices and consumers' fears of a financial squeeze, many people assert a nice Christmas is out of the picture this year. But I say "Not so!" Here are a few ideas to help make Christmas memorable without breaking the bank!

Go Potluck! You buy the turkey -- Have everyone else bring the side dishes and drinks. Turkeys in our area are .39/lb this time of year. If you buy just the turkey, it will only cost you about $5-$10 to feed everyone for a large family gathering.

Celebrate Christmas the week after Christmas. Take advantage of the after Christmas sales and plan your large extended family gathering for the week after Christmas. Besides being less expensive, it is unlikely to interfere with anyone else's Christmas plans.

Don't give gifts or give inexpensive gifts to hairstylists, babysitters, teachers and others. I found several wonderful small scented jar candles on clearance for .25 each. I will put three of them in a small basket (purchased at the thrift store for .25) with some tissue paper, ribbon and nice note. A great gift for $1.25!

Break up gift sets. If you find an item that comes in a gift set at Christmas, give parts of it to different recipients. This is great for bath or perfume sets.

Yard sales and thrift stores equal great savings. You can find a lot of new or nearly new items for pennies on the dollar. For our son, we found a working telescope in the box. It cost $1.00, so we saved $24! He got what he wanted and we didn't have to take out a home equity loan!

Make memories, not more junk. Most kids get more than plenty for Christmas from grandparents, aunts and uncles. If you can only afford one gift for your child, make it a memory! Wrap a note in a box with instructions for a treasure hunt. Send your child all over the house with clues and then have the real gift sitting under the tree when they return. Simple, but a great memory for them!

Christmas Tips and Ideas

* **Keep things as simple as possible.** If you find that you are unable to manage the twenty-five different cookie recipes you want to make, pick two or three of your specialties and just make large batches of those. Don't serve fifteen different dishes for Christmas dinner. Just do the five or six favorites.

* **Take scraps of fabric or felt and cut into Christmas shapes.** You can do this by using cookie cutters or templates. Then attach them to twine, wire or ribbon and use for garland all over the house or on your tree.

* **When stringing popcorn for garland,** let it sit for a couple of days to get stale. Stale popcorn is easier to string. (I sure wish I'd known that last year! We made popcorn and cranberry garland. It was very pretty!)

* **Put some vegetable oil on a rag and polish red and green apples.** Place in a bowl and fill in the spaces with greenery.

* **Wrap some of the pictures you have hanging on the wall to look like packages.** This can be a really cute and inexpensive addition to your decorations!

* **Send your Christmas packages early.** This may seem like an obvious tip, but many people don't do it. You can save a huge amount of money by doing this. Not only will you save money, but the more things you can get done and out of the way early, the fewer things you will have to do all at once at the last minute when too many tasks are already stressing you out!

* **When you have to send things through the mail,** think about what you'll buy. Is it fragile, heavy or very large? None of these are good candidates for shipping. (Some of our family spend $150 in shipping to mail $100 worth of gifts.) Instead send smaller items like videos, CDs, or books, which can be sent inexpensively by Media Mail. If you're OK with gift certificates, you can usually send them for the price of one stamp.

* **Do you like to have fresh greenery in your home for Christmas?** Go to any place that sells Christmas trees (tree lots, Lowe's, Wal-Mart,

etc.) and ask for the branches and cuttings that have fallen off. They are usually glad to get them off of their hands since they're just going to throw them away. Besides using them for decorations, try tucking them in and around your artificial tree to give it that fresh tree smell. (We sometimes go to a local park after a windy day and collect freshly fallen evergreen boughs.)

* For the kids' table at Christmas or just to use as a cute decoration, put a candle in a glass jar or bowl. Fill the rest of the bowl around the bottom of the candle with cinnamon candies, peppermints, nuts or colored gum balls or jaw breakers.

* I like decorating my house in a Candyland theme each year. If you have the same type of theme, at each place setting for dinner, decorate a small glass jar with a ribbon around it and fill it with multi-colored candy. This not only adds to the table decorations, but you can write the person's name on the jar and make it a small gift for him or her to take home.

* One of our traditions at Christmas is to always dress up. After all, we are celebrating Jesus' birthday, and in the same way that we would dress our very best if we were invited to the birthday party of the Queen of England or the President, why do any less for Christ's birthday? Besides, dressing up adds to the fun!

* Buy your Christmas tree after December 15th when they are much less expensive.

* Instead of a fancy tree skirt, use a white sheet. The colored gifts look great against the white. (Then your seven year old can wear the tree skirt herself like ours did! ;-)

* Don't worry about the extra expense of a "tree extender". They don't really work. Your tree just needs lots and lots of water. Make sure the cut end is always under water or it'll seal itself shut and stop drinking. Check often! Your tree may drink gallons of water in the first few days.

* Go to your carpet store and ask for the cardboard cores that carpet comes on. I wrap them in white plastic trash bags and twist red ribbon around them. That way I have instant giant peppermint sticks for my outside decorations (and they don't cost $50 each like the ones in the stores).

* Are some of your Christmas decorations and ornaments looking a little battle-scarred and worn? Maybe you want to change from the country look to a more sophisticated look. Try spray-painting your older things with gold, silver or copper paint.

* Recycle that artificial tree that you don't want any more. Bend the branches and connect them to make either one very large wreath or several small ones. If you're not ready to part with an artificial tree, you can still watch at garage sales for inexpensive trees to use for wreaths in the coming year.

* If you send a lot of cards each year, consider sending postcards instead of Christmas cards. They are less expensive to buy and cost less to send. You can even recycle some of the fronts of old Christmas cards to use as postcards.

* Got more eggnog than you can drink? Use leftover eggnog for French toast. Just add a little cinnamon to it and it works wonderfully.

You make the beds, you do the dishes, and six months later you have to start all over again.

- Joan Rivers

Homemade Gifts and
Other Such Things

If you have gone to the trouble to make someone homemade gifts, go the extra mile and make the presentation and packaging special too. It can make the difference between an "oh, thank you" gift and a "how cute is this, I love it, it's adorable!" gift.

* If you are giving cocoa mix in a mug tie peppermint sticks or candy canes onto the mug to use for stirring. Even one or two spoons dipped in white chocolate can make the difference between a "ho-hum" gift and a "wow!" gift.

* Copy the packaging and presentation ideas you see in magazines or on TV. There is a reason they can sell $.50 worth of cocoa for $25.

* Instead of just giving someone a plate of brownies, cut them into Christmas shapes with your cookie cutters. Things like stars, trees or bells work well. Go a step further and covering them with frosting or sprinkles.

* Take everyone's favorite rice crispy treats and cut them into shapes with your cookie cutters. There is even Christmas cereal available now. Try using that instead of regular rice crispies or add red or green food coloring to spruce up the rice crispies. Make a separate batch of red and green rice crispies before making the rice crispy treats.

* Instead of giving someone a plate of cookies, buy cellophane bags to put them in and tie with extra pretty ribbons. You can get clear cellophane bags at party stores or flower shops.

* When giving cookies, put a different twist on them by pressing a lollipop or popsicle stick into them before you bake them. If you use a popsicle stick, personalize it by writing the person's name or a special message on the stick. Once again, do something cute for a package. Slip them into a cellophane bag or cover with colored cellophane paper and tie with a bow. You can get lollipop or popsicle sticks at any discount store in the crafts or cake decorating section.

* Tie little jingle bells to the ends of the ribbon you use on your package or just for fun, put your gift in a box before you wrap it and throw in a couple of hands full of wrapped peppermints or Christmas candy.

Here are some recipes for homemade decorations, which also make great gifts:

Scented Cinnamon Ornaments

1 cup cinnamon
1 Tbsp. cloves
1 Tbsp. nutmeg
3/4 cup applesauce
2 Tbsp. white glue
   ribbon

In a bowl, mix the spices. Add applesauce and glue, stirring until well blended. Work mixture until dough is smooth and ingredients are thoroughly mixed. Divide into 4 portions and roll each portion on floured surface to 1/4 inch thickness. Cut dough with cookie cutters of desired shapes. Using a straw or toothpick, make a small hole in the top of each ornament. Place on wire racks and allow to dry at room temperature for several days. (For more uniform drying, turn ornaments over once each day.) Thread ribbon through holes to form garland. You can also glue to a wooden hoop, forming a wreath and decorate with ribbon as desired. Makes approximately 32 two-inch ornaments. DO NOT EAT!

Clay Christmas Ornaments

4 cups flour
1 cup salt
1 tsp. powdered alum
1 1/2 cups water

Mix ingredients well in a large bowl. If the dough is too dry, work in another tablespoon of water with your hands. Dough can be rolled or molded and can be colored with a few drops of food coloring.

To roll: Roll dough 1/8 inch thick on lightly floured board. Cut with cookie cutters dipped in flour. Insert wire or make hole in top about 1/4 inch down for hanging.

To mold: Shape dough no more than 1/2 inch thick.

Bake ornaments on ungreased cookie sheet for 30 minutes in 250° oven. Turn and bake another 1 1/2 hours until hard and dry. Remove and cool. When done, paint and seal with spray varnish. You can lightly sand before painting to make the paint adhere better.

*Alum can be found in the spice section of your store.

**Santa Claus has the right idea.
Visit people only once a year.**

- Victor Borge

Gift Ideas to Keep You From Becoming a Basket Case!

Need Gift Ideas for Christmas but don't want to spend a lot? Here are some tips to help you remember your friends without breaking the bank:

* **Buy items in sets and divide them among the baskets.** Buy a four pack of nail polish for four ladies baskets or buy packs of whistles or other party favors for the kids. Take individual popcorn, coffee or cocoa packets out of their boxes. They will fill the baskets better.

* **Shop garage sales and thrift stores** for baskets and other containers

* **Dollar stores have lots of great inexpensive gift ideas.** Browse!

* **Use cellophane bags to package your mixes.** They are inexpensive when purchased at party stores or florists.

* **A gift can be as simple as tea bags** in a tea cup tied with a pretty ribbon. A large soup mug and saucer with soup mix or a small glass bowl with some potpourri might also make a simple but nice gift.

Try making these specialty gift baskets:

Football Fan- (teenage boys, brothers, fathers and brothers-in-law!) Fill a large bowl purchased at the dollar store with candy bars, bags of microwave popcorn, sodas, chips, dips, a favorite football flag or hat, and a calendar of game days.

Fisherman- In a tackle box or fish bowl put hooks, bait, line, hot chocolate or sodas, trail mix, gloves, fishing magazines and a fish pillow.

Dog- In a dog bowl, place a ball, old sock with a knot tied in it, dog bones, rawhides, a leash, a name tag and a brush. You might include a picture of a mailman with "the enemy" written on it.

Cat- In a cat litter box, place a catnip toy, cat food, a poop scoop, a leash, a name tag and a little rubber mouse.

Car- In a large bucket, place fuzzy dice, air freshener, wax, car wash, chamois ("Shammy"), tire cleaner, a car trash can, a key ring, ice melter for cars and an ice scraper.

Baby Basket- Spray paint a basket white and line it with a baby blanket or use a diaper bag. Fill with bibs, baby oil, baby lotion, baby powder, diaper ointment, a teething ring, burp cloths, wipes and a rattle.

Relaxing Basket- Line a basket with a hand towel. Add a lavender candle, bath oil or bubble bath, bath salts, a favorite magazine or book, a poof and scented soap, and a do not disturb sign (Make one out of a piece of cardboard.).

Coffee Lover- In a basket, include flavored coffee packets, cinnamon sticks dipped in chocolate, wrapped in cellophane and tied with a ribbon, cookie mix or cookies, flavored powdered creamer and a coffee cup. Baker's Delight - Line a large mixing bowl with a dish towel. Add cookie mixes, hot chocolate mixes, brownie mix, muffin mix, a package of walnuts, measuring cups and pot holders.

Ice Cream Lover- Place tissue paper on the bottom of a basket. Add sundae dishes, an ice cream scoop, nuts, hot fudge sauce, butterscotch sauce, chocolate syrup, Maraschino cherries and a gift certificate for 2 1/2 gallons of ice cream.

Soup Basket- In a basket, stock pot or bean crock, add large soup mugs, 7 bean soup, cornbread mix, cookie mix and oyster crackers wrapped in cellophane bags and tied with a ribbon.

Nail Polish Basket- In a pretty bucket or basket, add a variety of nail polish, emery boards, nail clippers, polish remover, cotton balls, hand cream, cuticle cream and a nail buffer.

Family Night- In a large bowl, add a puzzle or game, popcorn, candy bars, soda, hot chocolate mix and mugs.

Fruit Basket- Line a basket with tissue paper. Add apples, oranges, hot chocolate mix, various teas and dried fruits (like figs or raisins). Sprinkle nuts on top of everything.

Cookie Delight- In a basket lined with tissue paper, add two cookie mixes in cellophane bags or jars tied with ribbons, Russian Tea (also in a cellophane bag or small jar tied with ribbon), cookie cutters, a teacup and two pot holders.

Chocolate Lover- In a basket, add Hot Chocolate Mix, Brownie Mix , Chocolate Peanut Butter Cookie Mix, Party Mints, Mexican Hot Chocolate Mix and a small package of marshmallows.

Hot Chocolate Mix

8 cups dry milk
4 3/4 cups powdered sugar
1 3/4 cups cocoa
1 1/2 cup non-dairy creamer
1 sm. pkg. instant chocolate pudding mix

Sift the ingredients into a large bowl. Place the mix into an airtight containers.

Attach this to the jar:

Hot Chocolate
5 Tbsp. (1/3 cup) Hot Chocolate Mix
1 cup hot water (not boiling)
marshmallows or whipped cream

Place the Hot Chocolate Mix into a mug. Add boiling water. Stir until Hot Chocolate mix is dissolved. Garnish as desired with marshmallows or whipped cream. Serves 1.

Apple Cinnamon Muffin Mix

2 cups flour
1/2 tsp. baking soda
1/4 tsp. salt
1 tsp. baking powder
1 tsp. ground cinnamon
1/2 cup raisins and/or nuts

In a bowl, mix together first 5 ingredients. Place in an air tight container. Package raisins and nuts separately.

Topping
3 Tbsp. sugar
1/4 tsp. cinnamon
1/4 tsp. nutmeg

Mix topping ingredients in a bowl. Package in a small cellophane bag.

Attach this to the jar:

Apple Cinnamon Muffin Mix

To prepare, preheat oven to 350°.
Mix together:
Apple Cinnamon Muffin Mix
raisins and/or nuts
1 cup apple juice
2 Tbsp. oil
1/2 cup applesauce
margarine, melted

Stir just until combined. Spoon into lightly greased muffin tins and bake for 20-25 minutes or until toothpick inserted in center comes out clean. While still warm, dip in melted margarine and then topping. Makes 12-15 muffins.

Save Big During After Christmas Sales!
(The most wonderful time of the year!)

Since Christmas is almost here, I thought I'd share some ways you can use after Christmas sales to help make next Christmas and occasions throughout the year financially easier.

After Christmas sales can be a great way to save money on things you would buy anyway, without paying full price. As you see the things that are on sale, try to predict which of those things you are likely to need during the next year.

Don't limit your thinking to Christmas! Consider how you may use after Christmas items for other occasions in the coming year. Be creative!

Don't go crazy and buy everything they have just because it is marked down. If you buy 20 of something you don't need and eventually just get rid of it, you didn't really save by getting it on clearance.

If you want to get some great deals but you also want a lot of selection, you'll want to show up in the store pretty early on December 26th. You can get deeper discounts if you wait several days or a week for the stores to mark items all the way down to 75% off. The down side of waiting is that the item you want may be gone if you wait too long. If you really have to have it, you probably want to get it sooner rather than wait.

If there's something that you want at Wal-Mart, you will definitely want to get there the first thing on December 26th because Wal-Mart attracts the die hard after Christmas shoppers who buy like hungry locusts. ;-)

You can often find good buys at grocery and drug stores a week or two after Christmas because there's not as much demand for after Christmas items in those stores.

Here are some of the things to consider as you visit after Christmas sales:

   * Buy new Christmas decorations for next year. This seems obvious to some of us, but if you've never thought about it, you can usually

213

get lights, lawn decorations, indoor decorations and other holiday-specific items for 50-75% off right after Christmas. We like to add to our display every year and it is much less expensive to buy after Christmas this year rather than before Christmas next year. Even our Christmas tree was a 50% off after Christmas buy. (Don't try this with live trees! They don't keep well! ;-)

* **Buy "Baby's First Christmas" items** (pajamas, bibs, ornaments, etc.) for those friends and relatives expecting babies in the next year.

* **Purchase holiday craft items.** Christmas ribbons, needlework, and other craft supplies are often marked down to 75% off. Get started on those projects and get them done early. Don't forget to get enough red ribbon and craft supplies for Valentines day.

* **Buy your red Valentine's Day and green St. Patrick's Day candy** on clearance after Christmas.

* **Christmas isn't just red and green any more.** You can get every color under the rainbow now. If you are decorating a room or having a special party, such as an anniversary you can purchase your supplies for 75% off. I've also purchased things like specialty lights for my son who collects anything that will light up.

* **Purchase gifts for next Christmas, birthdays, Mother's Day, Father's Day and teachers' gifts.** You can often find wonderful gift bath sets that make great gifts for teachers at 50% off. There are also bath sets for kids, make up sets for girls and cologne and perfume for men and women that you can give for any occasion. I purchase several extra girls and boys gifts sets for the kids to take to birthday parties. I buy hubby's cologne for the year (again, as a gift set) and give it to him on Father's Day. My sister in law liked a particular large red candle that I happened to notice was on sale after Christmas. I purchased it for $2 instead of the $10 regular price.

* **If you have a wedding coming up,** look for decorations with your wedding colors after Christmas. You can also get tablecloths and napkins for your household on clearance after Christmas. You can buy these at up to 75% off and use them every day.

* **Look for wrapping paper for other occasions.** Stores have colored and white tissue paper and wrapping paper that isn't necessarily just for Christmas. You can also buy Christmas paper for next to nothing after Christmas and save it for next Christmas or use it white side out for other holidays.

* **I buy the pre-packaged gingerbread kits** that are now available for my kids. For $2 each, it is much easier to have the house already baked and rolled out. I save them for the kids to decorate next year. (Of course we don't eat them.)

I buy about 3/4 of my gift items for the year the days and weeks after Christmas. By doing this, I save hundreds of dollars on gifts over the year.

(Kellam) Family Vacation

A couple with three children waited in line at San Francisco's Pier 41 to purchase tickets for a boat trip to Alcatraz.

Others watched with varying degrees of sympathy and irritation as the young children fidgeted, whined, and punched one another. The frazzled parents reprimanded them to no avail.

Finally they reached the ticket window.

"Five tickets, please," Dad said. "Two round trip, three one way."

PENNY PARENTING COLUMN –

(Author Unknown)

Thoughts From 1959

"I'll tell you one thing, if things keep going the way they are, it's going to be impossible to buy a week's groceries for $20."

"Have you seen the new cars coming out next year? It won't be long before $5000 will only buy a used one."

"Did you hear the post office is thinking about charging a dime just to mail a letter?"

"When I first started driving, who would have thought gas would someday cost 50 cents a gallon. Guess we'd be better off leaving the car in the garage."

"I never thought I'd see the day all our kitchen appliances would be electric. They are even making electric typewriters now."

"Next thing you know, the government will start paying us not to grow crops."

"I'm just afraid the Volkswagen car is going to open the door to a whole lot of foreign business."

"The drive in restaurant is convenient in nice weather, but I seriously doubt they will ever catch on."

"There is no sense going to Lincoln or Omaha anymore for a weekend. It costs nearly $15 a night to stay in a hotel."

"No one can afford to be sick any more, $35 a day in the hospital is too rich for my blood."

"I don't know about you but if they raise the price of coffee to 15 cents, I'll just have to drink mine at home."

"If they think I'll pay 50 cents for a hair cut, forget it. I'll have my wife learn to cut hair."

"We won't be going out much any more. Our baby sitter informed us she wants 50 cents an hour. Kids think money grows on trees."

Index of Recipes

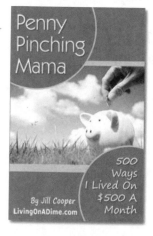

Keeping It Clean

This e-book series includes 3 e-books to help you **conquer the laundry pile, get your house in order and reduce your stress** with better organization.

Learn more at http://www.livingonadime.com/store

Dig Out Of Debt

Ready to get out of debt for good? It is easier than you think!

Don't let your debt make you feel powerless anymore! Use these proven strategies to change your thinking and help you eliminate your debt once and for all!

http://www.livingonadime.com/store

Free "Five Simple Steps To Save $500 A Month On Your Grocery Budget" mini e-course!

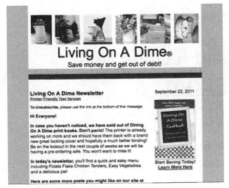

Sign up for our Free Newsletter and get the e-course free! You'll receive tips for saving money and getting out of debt plus learn how to save over $7000 in one year when you sign up now at:

http://www.livingonadime.com/newsletter-signups/

To order online

Print Books:

Dining On A Dime Cookbook, Eat Better Spend Less
Menus From Dining On A Dime
Quick And Easy Menus On A Dime
Penny Pinching Mama
Dig Out Of Debt

E-Books:

Dining On A Dime Cookbook
Groceries On A Dime
Penny Pinching Mama
Dig Out Of Debt e-Book series
Menus On A Dime e-Book Series
Pretty for Pennies
Moving On A Dime
Gifts In A Jar
Saving With Kids e-Book Series
Valentine's Day On A Dime
Winning The Credit Card Game
Halloween On A Dime

For online orders or free frugal tips and recipes visit
www.LivingOnADime.com

Order Form

Please send me:

___ copies **Dig Out Of Debt**	$17.95 ea	$_____
___ copies **Dining On A Dime Cookbook**	$21.95 ea	$_____
___ copies **Penny Pinching Mama**	$12.95 ea	$_____
___ copies **Menus From Dining On A Dime**	$ 7.95 ea	$_____

Shipping & Handling (**US Only**)	1 book $4.50	$_____
	each additional book $1.00	$_____
	Subtotal	$_____
Colorado Residents add 2.9 % Sales Tax		$_____
	Total	$_____

* Canadian Orders Triple Postage

Please enclose check payable to *Living on A Dime.*

<u>Ship To:</u>

Name_____

Address_____Apt. #____

City_____State ___Zip_____

Email Address_____ Phone_____

(Please include in case there is a problem with your order, we do not sell our
customers email addresses or phone numbers)

<u>Mail To:</u>

Living On A Dime
P.O. Box 193
Mead, CO 80542

Credit card orders may be placed online at:
<u>www.LivingOnADime.com</u>

Order Form

Please send me:

___ copies **Dig Out Of Debt**	$17.95 ea	$_____
___ copies **Dining On A Dime Cookbook**	$21.95 ea	$_____
___ copies **Penny Pinching Mama**	$12.95 ea	$_____
___ copies **Menus From Dining On A Dime**	$ 7.95 ea	$_____

Shipping & Handling (**US Only**)   1 book $4.50 $_____

each additional book $1.00 $_____

Subtotal $_____

Colorado Residents add 2.9 % Sales Tax $_____

Total $_____

* Canadian Orders Triple Postage

Please enclose check payable to *Living on A Dime.*

Ship To:

Name_____

Address_____Apt. #___

City_____State ___Zip_____

Email Address_____ Phone_____

(Please include in case there is a problem with your order, we do not sell our customers email addresses or phone numbers)

Mail To:
Living On A Dime
P.O. Box 193
Mead, CO 80542

Credit card orders may be placed online at:
www.LivingOnADime.com

Order Form

Please send me:

____ copies **Dig Out Of Debt** $17.95 ea $_____

____ copies **Dining On A Dime Cookbook** $21.95 ea $_____

____ copies **Penny Pinching Mama** $12.95 ea $_____

____ copies **Menus From Dining On A Dime** $ 7.95 ea $_____

Shipping & Handling (**US Only**)   1 book $4.50 $_____

         each additional book $1.00 $_____

             Subtotal $_____

   Colorado Residents add 2.9 % Sales Tax $_____

              Total $_____

* Canadian Orders Triple Postage

Please enclose check payable to ***Living on A Dime.***

<u>Ship To:</u>

Name_____

Address_____Apt. #____

City_____State ___Zip_____

Email Address_____ Phone_____

(Please include in case there is a problem with your order, we do not sell our customers email addresses or phone numbers)

<u>Mail To:</u>
Living On A Dime
P.O. Box 193
Mead, CO 80542

Credit card orders may be placed online at:
<u>www.LivingOnADime.com</u>